D0123552

Praises for Celebrate Simply

"Finally, a book that gives real-life advice to address the real-life problems of holiday stress and overspending! If you're tired of celebrations that leave you yearning for something more, do yourself a favor by reading this book. Not only will *Celebrate Simply* teach you how to save money; it will also show you how to enrich and add meaning to your celebrations as well."

Dave Ramsey
Host of *The Dave Ramsey Show* and best-selling author of *Financial Peace* and *More than Enough*

"You simply must read this book if you want to make your special days more meaningful. Nancy Twigg will help you cut costs without cutting the joy of family celebrations."

David and Claudia Arp
Authors of *10 Great Dates* and *Answering the 8 Cries of the Spirited Child* and founders of Marriage Alive

"Buried in the stress of holidays and celebrations? Here's the perfect book that shows how to really enjoy them again— without the commercial complexity, and with a whole lot of meaning."

Janet Luhrs
Author of *The Simple Living Guide*, *Simple Loving*, and editor of *Simple Living Oasis*

"Nancy Twigg understands that celebrations are about joy. She also knows that we experience joyful celebrations all too rarely. To change things we've got to start talking with one another— probing the true meaning of our celebrations and coming to understand unrealistic expectations. To start the conversation, why not give people Nancy's book?"

Cecile Andrews
Author of *The Circle of Simplicity: Return to the Good Life*

"My middle name is 'Keep It Simple' and this book certainly does that. You will have the tools to reduce your stress during the holiday season. This book is a guide for simplifying your holidays and at the same time make them more meaningful."

Emilie Barnes
Author and Speaker

"...Well-designed with boxed quotes, lists, an index and resource section, the book is easy to read and easy to use as a reference guide. Nancy helps us to avoid stress and debt and to focus on relationships instead of stuff when we celebrate. We recommend it so highly that we plan make it available in our national Resource Guide and web site."

Gerald Iversen
National Coordinator, Alternatives for Simple Living

"Nancy has taken her expertise and made a wonderful tool for people! With her help, you can still celebrate all aspects of life without it taking your wallet or time to the cleaners."

Jonni McCoy
Author and founder of *Miserly Moms*

"The most meaningful celebrations come from opening your heart, not emptying your wallet. This book will save you money, save your sanity, and in many cases, save your relationships."

Michael Webb
Author of *The RoMANtic's Guide* and founder of TheRomantic.com

"*Celebrate Simply* is a gem—packed with practical information, personal anecdotes, and excellent suggestions for not only surviving, but also thriving in the midst of every holiday season."

Rhonda Barfield
Author of *Feed Your Family For $12 A Day*, *Real-Life Homeschooling*, and *15-Minute Cooking*

"Simply the best book ever on simplifying holidays and special occasions throughout the year. Nancy Twigg has created an indispensable guide that should be on every family's shelf!"

Deborah Taylor-Hough
Author of *Frugal Living For Dummies* and Editor *of The Simple Times* Newsletter

"A practical book that is engaging, informative, *and* inspiring. A great gift for yourself and your friends."

Dru Scott Decker
Author of *Finding More Time in Your Life*

"…From Christmas to birthdays, saving money to building traditions, making memories to sparking your creativity, Nancy covers it all. Her easy-to-read style guides even the most challenged gift-giver with more than enough ideas, suggestions and answers for any occasion."

Karon Goodman
Author of *The Stepmom's Guide to Simplifying Your Life* and several other books

"This book is for all those who wish to regain sanity in their celebrations. Nancy confronts and dispels many of the unwritten rules of gift giving as well as providing many wise and creative alternatives to running up the credit card."

Angie Zalewski
Co-founder of the Frugal Family Network, Inc.
Co-author of *Cheap Talk with the Frugal Friends*

"Joyful living is what *Celebrate Simply* is all about. Nancy shows us all that living joyfully does not have to be stressful or expensive. *Celebrate Simply* is a practical guide to experiencing the best life has to offer!"

Rowland Buck
Pastor, Ebenezer United Methodist Church
(Knoxville, TN)

"Nancy Twigg's book is the definitive book for saving money and memories during holiday celebrations throughout the year. Her readable style is delightful and the extensive research is evident throughout this incredible book..."

Ellie Kay
Author of *Shop, Save and Share* and *Money Doesn't Grow on Trees*

"Celebrate Simply" is simply wonderful! Nancy provides a wealth of ideas to establish Christian family traditions to strengthen home and family. This is a great resource book for those striving to return to simple, meaningful family occasions, while being mindful of their budgets."

Nikki Willhite
AllThingsFrugal.com

"What a gift Nancy has given to each of us! *Celebrate Simply* brings the confidence to celebrate in simpler and affordable ways while enriching each holiday in meaningful and traditional ways. *Celebrate Simply* is a book to be passed down through the generations."

Kim S. Crabill
Founder and President of Roses and Rainbows Ministries, Inc.

"Celebrate Simply" will help you find the meaning of Christmas and also help you find your pocketbook again."

Tawra Kellam
Editor, www.notjustbeans.com

"From front to back and every page in between, this book is a wonderful example of how to celebrate each special occasion with simplicity and sincerity. Nancy has outdone herself in this book by covering every aspect of celebrating. Every home should have a copy of this wonderful resource!"

Pearl Sanborn
Publisher of *Heart and Home Newsletter*

"Practical tools for returning the joy to your holidays."
Gary Foreman
Editor of *The Dollar Stretcher*

"*Celebrate Simply* is a packed with excitement. Twigg has included a whole trunkful of suggestions, and writes with understanding for families who want to simplify their holidays while boosting their sense of festivity. I would recommend this book to families, churches and party planners—in fact, to anyone who wants to keep a sense of holiday cheer while holding down the cost and the work."
Kristen Ingram
Author of twenty books and writing instructor for the Writer's Digest School

"Get ready to have your life restored as Nancy Twigg rejuvenates your holidays with sound strategies, practical principles, and a healthy dose of common sense. In her humorous style, Mrs. Twigg gives you real ammo as you conquer those holiday monsters that siphon all your time and energy."
Jill Bond
Author of *Mega Cooking* and *Dinner's in the Freezer!*

"Celebrations do not have to involve an excess of spending and stress to be a success. *Celebrate Simply* provides realistic plans to make special occasions more meaningful and enjoyable for everyone. By following the practical advice in this book, you can infuse holidays with meaning without overextending yourself physically and financially."
Cynthia Sumner
Author of *Time Out for Mom...Ahhh Moments* and *Planes, Trains, and Automobiles...With Kids!*

"Nancy Twigg brings back the joy of celebrating with her practical and economical ideas in *Celebrate Simply*."
Joyce Frye
Author of *Mommy Tracker*

Celebrate Simply:
Your Guide to Simpler,
More Meaningful Holidays
and Special Occasions

Copyright © 2003 Nancy Twigg.
First Edition, Second Print Run (September 2003)

Published by Counting the Cost Publications.

All rights reserved. No part of this publication may be reproduced, stored in a retrieval system, or transmitted in any form or by any means, electronic, mechanical, recording or otherwise—except by a reviewer who may quote brief passages in a review to be printed in a magazine, newspaper or on the Web—without the prior written permission of the publisher. For information, please contact Counting the Cost Publications, 8715 Brucewood Lane, Knoxville TN 37923.

PRINTED IN THE UNITED STATES OF AMERICA

ISBN 0-9728396-0-7
LCCN 2003090627

The information and ideas in this book are offered as general suggestions only. The author and publisher have taken precautions to ensure that the content is accurate and trustworthy. Readers should exercise judgment in deciding whether a particular piece of advice is appropriate and applicable for use in their own circumstances.

ATTENTION CORPORATIONS, ORGANIZATIONS AND CHURCH GROUPS: Quantity discounts are available on bulk purchases of this book for educational or gift purposes, for use as premiums or for fundraiser sales. Special books or book excerpts can also be created to fit specific needs. For information, contact Counting the Cost Publications, 8715 Brucewood Lane, Knoxville TN 37923. Email: books@countingthecost.com

Ashton Miller, Editor
Cover design by Holly Smith, www.bookskins.net

Text Printed on Recycled Paper

Celebrate Simply:
Your Guide to Simpler,
More Meaningful Holidays
and Special Occasions

Nancy Twigg

Dedication

This book is humbly dedicated to my amazing husband and best friend for life, Michael. *With you and your love, every day is a celebration.*

To my precious daughter, Lydia Grace. *The day we learned you were coming is a surprise I will celebrate for the rest of my life.*

To my incredible parents and parents-in-law, Bill and Dorothy Gardner and Bruce and Carol Twigg. *Cheers to you for shaping us into what we are so that we can shape Lydia into what she will become.*

And to my awesome Heavenly Father. *I know you are planning the biggest family celebration ever. I can't wait until the day the victory party begins!*

Acknowledgements

A special thanks goes to Chip Miller who gave my manuscript his expert "attention" and "care" and taught me not to use so many "quotation marks." (Sorry, Chip—I couldn't resist!) Thanks also to his wife, Melanie, for her encouragement and for allowing Chip to take time away from family activities to help me. Much appreciation goes to Pastor Rowland Buck and Judy Pierson as well for their help with the proofreading process.

I am also indebted to Deborah Taylor-Hough, author of *A Simple Choice: A Practical Guide for Saving Your Time, Money and Sanity*; Michael Webb, author of *The RoMANtic's Guide: Hundreds of Creative Tips for a Lifetime of Love*; and Karon Goodman, author of *The Stepmom's Guide to Simplifying Your Life*. Thanks to each of you for giving me the guidance and nudges I needed to move from wanting to write a book to actually doing it.

And to many faithful friends and *Counting the Cost* subscribers, especially my prayer partner Angel Ayala, thank you for all the prayers and encouraging words you offered during the writing of this book. Your support upheld me more than you'll ever know.

Table of Contents

Introduction

*H*ave you ever longed for more meaningful holidays? Do you often feel overwhelmed by all the planning and shopping and spending and wrapping and wish that celebrations didn't have to be so complicated? Do special occasions in your family frequently get out of hand tempting you to opt out completely?

If so, this book is for you. The message of this book is simple: Holidays don't have to be complex. They don't have to be stressful. The sentiment of the special day—whether it is Christmas, Easter, Mother's Day or Valentine's Day—doesn't have to get lost in the confusion of commercialization. There is another way, a better way. And that is what I want to share in this book.

An Out of Control Holiday Affair

Before we begin, let me share with you a little story. I call it, *The Tale of a Holiday Gone Horribly Wrong.* This account took place during the Christmas season, although it could have happened during any other holiday or special occasion.

It all started so innocently. The heroine of our story simply wanted to make the holiday something to remember for her family and friends. As a one-woman Christmas machine, she was determined to see that the Yuletide holidays were perfect for everyone that year. Great idea, right?

Wrong! What was meant to be Christmas magic quickly became Christmas mayhem. Her desire to have a wonderful Christmas soon became an obsession with orchestrating the *perfect* Christmas (if such a holiday even exists). Despite her best intentions, this poor woman's lofty aspirations siphoned the joy and spiritual significance right out of her family's holiday season.

Instead of a joyous occasion to look forward to, Christmas became a self-imposed deadline that she had to meet regardless of the personal consequences. By the weekend before Christmas, her family's Christmas tree was still undecorated because the woman was too busy making presents and planning lavish holiday meals to take time for this treasured family ritual. On the verge of total exhaustion, our heroine resembled a human time bomb ready to blow at any moment. When her poor unsuspecting husband tried to ease the tension by giving her an affectionate hug, she exploded.

"Don't touch me now. Can't you see how stressed I am?"

The rest of that awful day was spent in stony silence. All she wanted to do was make it a Christmas to remember, but now it seemed the memories would all be unpleasant. "If this Christmas was supposed to be perfect," she sulked, "why do I feel so rotten?"

Does this sound familiar? Have you ever been so caught up in the hype and hubbub that the true sentiment and cause for the occasion passed by you completely? I wish I could say the sad story I shared is just a tale I made up to illustrate my point. I also wish I could say the harried heroine is a fictitious character with any likeness to a real person being purely coincidental.

Unfortunately, neither of those statements is true. As much as I hate to admit it, I am the woman who single-handedly almost ruined Christmas for my family one year. I am the woman who made Dr. Seuss's Grinch look like a nice guy. Alas, I am the one who could have passed for Ebenezer Scrooge's twin sister.

What Went Wrong?

Oh, my intentions were noble, but my follow-through was pitifully off-kilter and out of whack. As I look back on this event in the Twigg family history, I can see several reasons for this self-inflicted disaster.

- ❑ Too much to do with too little time to do it
- ❑ Unrealistic expectations of what makes a celebration memorable
- ❑ Inordinate emphasis on gifts and food rather than spiritual reflection and quality time with family and friends

We'll talk more about these contributing factors later, but for now, the point is that my story is not uncommon. What happened in my family one Christmas happens frequently as families everywhere celebrate special occasions. Gift giving gets too expensive; simple family dinners quickly become ten-course meals. Husbands and wives bicker over where to spend the special day: with his parents, her parents, or at home where they both would rather be anyway. Quality family time gets lost in the shuffle and everyone ends up disappointed.

Let me assure you that there is a simpler, more meaningful route to holiday harmony. One that involves less stress and less expense. One that leaves family members exhilarated, not exhausted. I can't say that my family attains this harmony each and every time or that we never momentarily veer off course. But we have seen a glimpse of a beautifully simple and meaningful way of honoring the special events and seasons in our lives. We've crossed over to the simpler side of celebrating. We can joyfully say with full assurance, "Celebrations can be simple! They can be meaningful! They don't have to be stressful!"

My goal in writing this book is to present you with a treasure trove of ideas you can use to make your own family celebrations closer to what you truly want them to be. If reading these pages leaves you inspired to change the way you celebrate and equipped with new ideas to help you make those changes, *Celebrate Simply* has fulfilled its mission.

What You'll Find in This Book

If you asked one hundred people which holiday or special occasion they find most stressful and taxing, the majority would most likely answer Christmas. If you then asked what aspect of the Christmas season causes the greatest apprehension, the most common answer would probably be gift giving.

With this thought in mind, you will find that the longest chapters in this book deal with simplifying gift giving and the Christmas season. Each additional cause for celebration that is covered is addressed from the standpoint of how to simplify any unique aspects of that particular holiday. Because birthday and anniversary gift giving is something you are likely to do many times throughout the year, I have included a master list of all the gift ideas mentioned in this book in Chapter Nine: *Celebrating Birthdays and Anniversaries Simply* to serve as a quick reference. And, in case you don't find specific information on the particular special occasion you want to simplify, an index of holiday stress factors and corresponding page references can be found in Chapter Ten: *Conclusion.*

Now on to the simpler side of celebrations...

Chapter One:
Meaningful Gift Giving

*B*ecause gifts have become such an integral part of holiday celebrations in this country, let's start by examining and rethinking the whole gift giving process. One of the first steps in getting down to a meaningful holiday experience is finding compromise with your concept of what gift giving should be. A simplified approach to the holidays must include making peace with how and why you give gifts.

~ *Part I: The Whys and Hows of Giving Gifts* ~

"The Rules" of Gift Giving

I remember a very familiar time in my life prior to arriving at a more balanced approach to gift giving. Frequently I found that what I wanted to buy for that special someone, I couldn't afford. And what I could afford, I really didn't want to give as my gift. I recall searching for what seemed like hours for something I felt was both affordable and appropriate.

Everyone loves the idea of giving and receiving presents, but the problem is that there are so many unwritten rules about gift exchanges. And following all the rules can put you in the poorhouse fast. Let's take a look at a few of the rules and consider how breaking them might actually be a better, more thoughtful way to handle gift exchanges.

Rule 1: Gifts must be new. Who says a gift has to be new? Antiques and rare collectibles are examples of great gifts that aren't brand new. But even items that have been very gently used can be wonderful offerings if they are matched to the recipient's tastes, interests, and values. By buying secondhand, you can often purchase much nicer gifts than you could afford otherwise. With this thought in mind, yard sales are wonderful sources for brand-new and like-new merchandise that was never used or barely used by the original recipient. Although some may frown on the idea of giving gifts that come from yard sales, I can hardly see the difference between a like-new book or unopened gift set that came from a yard sale and one that was purchased at a department store. If a gift item is in good condition and fits the recipient perfectly, so what if it was purchased secondhand?

Rule 2: You must spend a certain amount on gifts. If you find a terrific bargain on a gift that seems perfect, you may actually feel a tinge of guilt for spending so little. I remember once hearing someone say, "If my relatives can't spend $25 on a gift for my wedding, they are just too cheap!" How sad that this young lady felt that way! The dollar amount you spend is not a barometer of how much you love or respect the recipient. Remember the perfect gift rule: If the item is something the recipient really wants or needs, it won't matter to her how much or how little you spend. In fact, if the recipient is also trying to watch her spending, she will probably admire your savvy shopping skills.

Rule 3: If someone gives you a gift, you must reciprocate. Inevitably there will be times when you receive a gift from someone who wasn't on your gift list. When this happens, you can either scramble awkwardly to reciprocate or just accept the gift graciously. In most cases, the giver would probably rather hear, "I'm sorry that I don't have anything for you, but I appreciate your kindness," than to know your gift to her was an afterthought motivated by guilt. This strange form of gift giving *quid pro quo* is flawed by its very nature. A gift is something given freely, with no strings attached.

Rule 4: There should be equality in gift giving. If someone gives you an expensive gift, do you feel badly for giving her something inexpensive? If so, why? There is a big difference between being cheap and being careful with your money. Being cheap is selfishly spending as little as possible without giving consideration to whether the item is something the recipient really wants or needs. In contrast, being careful with your money is showing your love with gifts that are within your means. Most likely, your friends and relatives wouldn't want you to spend more than you can comfortably afford anyway.

Don't Let the Rules Rule

Following all of the do's and don'ts of modern day gift giving quickly turns it into a compulsory, stress-invoking ritual rather than a voluntary display of goodwill and affection. Worrying if you gave the right gift, if it cost enough, and if you reciprocated every time you were expected to makes gift giving a drudgery. Holidays quickly lose their meaning when gift giving usurps its rightful place in the celebration and becomes the all-encompassing focus of the special occasion.

Not letting the rules rule you can be a formidable challenge. Pressures to conform from family, friends and society as a whole are powerful. You may feel like "the voice of one crying in the desert" if you suggest buying gifts from yard sales or setting a small spending limit. That is where the use of ingenuity and creativity come into play. If you can wow resistant family members with the thoughtful gifts you are able to give without spending a fortune, you will slowly but surely win over the skeptics.

> Holidays quickly lose their meaning when gift giving usurps its rightful place in the celebration and becomes the all-encompassing focus of the special occasion.

What is a Perfect Gift?

Let's take a little detour and talk for a minute about what makes a gift special. Have you ever given or received what you felt was a perfect gift? We all enjoy receiving gifts that are well-suited, and we hope recipients of gifts we give will utter those two little magic words, "It's perfect!" There is a sense of pride in knowing that your offering brought happiness to your loved one.

Certainly the desire to please is admirable, but keep in mind that this pressure to locate, select, purchase and bestow the perfect gift can take the joy right out of giving. What should be a positive, pleasurable experience turns into a pass-or-fail proposition. If the recipient expresses delight in your gift, you pass the gift giving test. If the color, size, shape or any other aspect of the present is not exactly what the receiver had in mind, you fail despite your best efforts and intentions.

> Even an inexpensive gift becomes memorable when the giver takes the time, care and consideration to determine what would mean a great deal to the recipient.

So what is a perfect gift? You chose to read this book because you want to simplify and take the stress out of holiday celebrations. A major step in the holiday simplification process is to rethink and redefine your concept of what makes a good gift. Think about gifts you have received that were particularly memorable. Most likely they were not the ones that carried the highest price tag.

The Bible gives us a beautiful example of meaningful gift giving in Mark 12:41-44. The setting for this story is the temple. Mark describes how Jesus carefully observed as worshippers dropped their offering gifts into the temple treasury. After watching many of the rich contribute substantial sums, He noticed a poor widow dropping in two small copper coins. Verse 42 (NIV) tells us that these coins were only worth a fraction of a penny, yet Jesus praised the woman for her generosity. Jesus told His disciples that the rich gave out of their abundance; they had plenty more at home so the gifts they gave meant little to them. The widow, on the other hand, had nothing else to give. Though small in monetary value, her gift was perfect because it was given out of great love and personal sacrifice.

In thinking back over the gifts I have received from my dear husband, Michael, over the years, a couple of items quickly stand out in my memory as perfect gifts. One was store-bought and one was homemade, but neither cost much to make or acquire. One of these gifts was a magazine that probably cost less than three dollars. What makes this magazine special is that it contained a short paragraph about the newsletter I publish. This happened back when the newsletter was just getting started, so the thought of national exposure was very exciting. When I learned that the magazine had mentioned my newsletter, I tried to find a copy of that particular issue but was unable to get my hands on one. Like a skilled detective, Michael searched and searched until he located one for me to find under the tree on Christmas morning.

The other gift was a handmade sliding extension shelf to fit my desk. At that time, my office was just a corner of our bedroom. It seemed I never had enough room on my desk to spread out. One day I casually mentioned that the desk I used at my old job had a pullout shelf that came in handy whenever I needed extra surface space. Because Michael is a skilled woodworker, it was easy for him to determine what modifications to my desk were needed to accommodate a sliding shelf, and then make the shelf out of wood. What a surprise when I opened the gift box and found a shelf like the one I offhandedly mentioned months before!

What makes both of these gifts extraordinary is that Michael gave attention to a need or desire I expressed rather than something I specifically asked for, and then figured out how he could fulfill that desire. This, I believe, is the key to giving a perfect gift: knowing enough about the person to figure out what she would enjoy. Often, as was the case with the two special gifts I mentioned, the gift that makes the biggest impression is not necessarily expensive. Even an inexpensive gift becomes memorable when the giver takes the time, care and consideration to determine what would mean a great deal to the recipient.

Have you ever noticed how difficult it is to choose a gift for someone you don't know very well? Sure, you can give something generic that would fit a wide range of people, but I've never felt good about giving one-size-fits-all presents. Meaningful gift giving is a product of knowing enough about the recipient's needs, tastes and values to know what would bring her pleasure.

Choosing Meaningful Gifts

Observing a need and then finding a way to fulfill it is one surefire way to make a lasting impression. Another way to win the heart of someone on your gift list is to give the recipient something she can't buy for herself. Handmade gifts are a good example. Even if the recipient could purchase something similar, it wouldn't be the same because it would lack the loving care you put into the gift you made yourself. Another example of gifts that fall into this category are things the recipient can't buy for herself because she is on a tight budget.

At other times, what makes a gift extraordinary is not the fact that the recipient couldn't buy the item for herself, but that she simply wouldn't. If the person is practical and frugal by nature, she may rarely spend money or time on things that aren't necessities. Little indulgences may seem too frivolous or self-indulgent for her to ever purchase on her own. Such items become extra special treats when given as a gift.

Another route to selecting a meaningful gift is to focus on what the receiver values. What new grandparent wouldn't love a gift that somehow incorporates a picture of the precious grandbaby? Or what aspiring young musician wouldn't enjoy a gift relating to the instrument she plays? If your gift somehow reflects what your loved one holds dear, you can bet it will be received with gratitude and pleasure.

As you think about the various avenues for choosing purposeful presents, you may wonder how this can be done inexpensively. Remember not to confuse price with value. A perfectly suited gift is still perfectly suited no matter how little it costs. Focusing only on how much a gift costs is materialism; focusing on the value of a present in the eyes of the recipient is thoughtful gift giving, expressive of your true feelings and intent.

A Grab Bag of Inexpensive Gift Ideas

If your family is on a limited budget, one major source of holiday and special occasion stress can be the burden that gift giving places on an already tight cash flow. I believe many people spend more than they can afford simply because they don't know better. They have no experience with using their creativity to come up with an offering that doesn't cost much but is truly useful, enjoyable and appreciated by the recipient. You may be one of these people.

Maybe you grew up in a family where handmade gifts were never given, or where special occasions were always preceded with hours of shopping in the local department store. If this is the case, you may feel inadequately equipped to face the challenge of frugal, yet thoughtful gift giving. If so, here is a list of low-cost ideas to free the flow of your own creative juices.

Free or Almost Free

❑ Write an IOU for something that the recipient usually pays to have done. Good examples are babysitting, cutting the grass, or giving a permanent wave.

❑ Using your computer, create a Certificate of Appreciation for being the world's best parent or going above and beyond the call of duty as a friend.

❑ Make a book of coupons for special treats such as breakfast in bed, car washes or unlimited talk time during which you provide a listening ear.

❑ Do you draw, compose music or write poetry? Create a piece of art in honor of your loved one.

❑ You probably already have an extra picture frame around the house that is not in use. Make it into a personalized gift by inserting a special family picture.

$5 or Less

- ❑ Give a gift certificate for a movie rental. Some video stores sell gift certificates in $5 increments.
- ❑ Using a camcorder, make a special videotape of the recipient's children or grandchildren. Have the kids sing songs and tell what they love most about the recipient.
- ❑ Make a gift basket filled with samples and other inexpensive items from yard sales, dollar stores, etc. Go with a theme or make it a mixture of various useful items.
- ❑ Buy an inexpensive photo album and gather some family pictures. Make up funny captions for each picture. Tape the captions beside the photos in the album.
- ❑ Make two batches of the recipient's favorite cookies. Put one batch in a decorative tin to be enjoyed now. Wrap the other batch in freezer bags to be frozen for later.

Up to $10

- ❑ Put together a basket of snacks for the person who spends a lot of time in front of the TV. Include gourmet popping corn, bags of chips and pretzels, nuts, etc.
- ❑ For the coffee lover, buy a pound of flavored coffee from a store specializing in gourmet coffees. Add a decorative mug from a dollar store.
- ❑ Pick up several different bubble baths, bath oils and body lotions from a dollar store. Arrange them in a pretty basket or in a festive gift bag.
- ❑ Check out the bargain bookrack at your local bookstore. Find a book on a topic of interest to the recipient.
- ❑ Create a "care basket" (a care package in a basket) filled with tissues, cold medicines, bandages, aspirin or any other common items that you know the recipient can use.
- ❑ Buy a book of stamps along with some stationery and a new pen from the dollar store.
- ❑ Buy a $10 gift card from the local grocery store so the recipient can enjoy a small splurge that she couldn't normally afford.

Economical Gift Ideas Especially for Young People

- ❏ Encourage creativity by giving items such as new crayons, markers, an art pad, sidewalk chalk, construction paper, etc. These can usually be purchased for a couple of dollars each. If you want to spend more, make a basket or gift bag filled with a variety of these items.

- ❏ Give a homemade gift certificate for a free trip to the ice cream shop or video arcade. You foot the bill for the ice cream or supply $5 in quarters for playing the games.

- ❏ Give the child on your list her own disposable camera along with an IOU for free film developing to use when she finishes taking all the pictures on the roll.

- ❏ Gift certificates for McDonald's, Baskin-Robbins or TCBY® make great gifts for children, teenagers or even college students who can't afford to go out very often.

- ❏ Make a large basket or bucket of the young person's favorite homemade cookies. If you want, include a note stating that the container may be returned for refills throughout the year.

~ *Part II: A Different Approach to Gift Giving* ~

The Gift Shelf

When it comes to gift giving, most people wait until the last minute to go shopping. With the gift giving occasion only days away, they search frantically for a gift. If luck is with them as they shop, they find something that is both appropriate and affordable. If luck is not with them, they usually overspend, buy something inappropriate or show up empty-handed for the gift giving occasion.

Does this sound familiar? Have you ever waited until the last minute and then scrambled to come up with an acceptable gift? If so, it doesn't have to be this way. Let me tell you about another approach to the gift giving scenario. This concept is certainly not original, as many people have shared with me that they do something similar. This idea can take many forms, but in our family, we call it the "Gift Shelf."

Of course, your gift shelf doesn't have to be a shelf at all. It could just as easily be a gift closet or gift cabinet. Whatever you call it, the idea is the same. Rather than waiting to shop until an occasion arises, you acquire gifts all year long, storing them in a designated place until the special occasion arrives.

This system of giving has many benefits. First, you can relax and enjoy special occasions without worrying about last minute shopping for gifts. The expenditure of time and money involved in gift giving is also spread out over the entire year. This benefit is especially important around the Christmas holidays when you have so many gifts to give within such a short time period. Gift giving becomes more manageable because you prepare for it a little at a time rather than all at once.

With this system, you have the option of taking your time in locating a perfectly suited item at a good price rather than frantically buying whatever you can find. And, if you keep your gift shelf well stocked, you can actually be more spontaneous in your giving. If a birthday sneaks up on you or a friend is having a rough day, one quick trip to your gift shelf easily produces a thoughtful gift for the unexpected occasion.

Maybe this technique is one you've used for years. If so, you already know what a lifesaver your gift stash can be. When I was first married, it was my dear husband who suggested that we start our gift shelf. He would often say, "This would make a good birthday gift for Mom," or "My brother would enjoy this for Christmas," when he found a bargain while we were out shopping or doing our weekly yard sale rounds. At first I thought, "Your mother's birthday is months away—why bother now?" I admit that I was a little slow to catch on, but when I finally saw the benefits of gifting in advance, I was hooked.

> By simply changing to a more proactive approach, you can easily put the joy back into what is supposed to be the joyous act of gift giving.

How to Start Your Own Gift Shelf

If you've never tried proactive gift buying, maybe this approach sounds good to you and you want to begin using it yourself. First, find a place to store your gifts. Under a bed, in your linen closet, in the attic—anywhere will do. We put our gifts in old copy paper boxes on the top shelf of our closet. Boxes of uniform size definitely come in handy for easy storage and stacking. Just be sure that the place you chose is safe from uninvited raids by family members or critters such as mice or insects. A friend of mine learned this lesson the hard way. She thought her attic was safe until a mouse ate all the chocolate she had stashed away for her children's Christmas stockings!

Next, begin collecting items for your gift shelf. Always be on the lookout for inexpensive items that would make good gifts. Flea markets, yard sales, clearance racks and going out of business sales are all great places to look. If you find something at a great price but don't know whom to give it to, buy it anyway to use for a party favor or hostess gift or a "just because" gift ("just because I love you," or "just because you're feeling down").

To get full benefit from your gift shelf, I suggest keeping an inventory of the gifts you acquire. Use your computer or a sheet of notebook paper to jot down each item you buy and the person to whom you plan to give it. Write down those extra gifts that aren't for anyone in particular, too. Each time you give a gift, be sure to mark it off your list. Certainly this is not totally necessary if keeping track of things is not your forte. However, I found that as my gift inventory grew to more than a couple of boxes, it was quite helpful to be able to see at a glance whose birthday or anniversary was taken care of and which family members were still in need of gifts.

Using this method, we now usually have family birthday presents purchased months in advance and can have almost all of our Christmas shopping done by Thanksgiving if we work at it. Some savvy shoppers who hit the after-Christmas sales may even have all of their gift shopping for the whole year done by the end of January. What a relief it is to know that we are prepared when a special occasion arises! By simply changing our approach, we were able to put the joy back into what is supposed to be the joyous act of gift giving.

~ *Part III: Homemade Gifts* ~

Make It Yourself Gift Baskets

In the past decade, gift baskets have become extremely popular. I believe this is because gift baskets provide such a versatile and economical means for giving thoughtful, personalized gifts. Florists and gift shops usually charge a hefty price for custom-made baskets. Thankfully, you can make gift baskets that are just as attractive for a fraction of the cost. All you need are a few basic supplies, inexpensive filler items and a healthy dose of creativity.

Supplies You Will Need

In addition to ordinary things like scissors and tape, there are only a few other necessary supplies. Most can be purchased very inexpensively.

- ❑ A basket – The basket you use can be plain and simple, or fancy and decorative. Yard sales and dollar stores are great sources for baskets. Or you may have baskets around the house from gifts you were given that you can reuse.
- ❑ Filler material – The grass used in Easter baskets works great or you can purchase similar material from a craft store. Better yet, make your own by shredding brown paper bags or brightly colored paper.
- ❑ Cellophane wrap – Although it is not necessary, wrapping your basket in clear or tinted cellophane makes it look like it came from a gift shop. Rolls of cellophane can be purchased from any craft store. Another attractive alternative is to use large pieces of tulle, the sheer mesh used for wedding veils which can be purchased at any fabric store. Using tulle adds a touch of elegance and is more economical than cellophane wrap.
- ❑ Ribbon – A bright, pretty bow also gives your gift basket a professional look. Ribbon can be purchased at yard sales or on clearance at craft and fabric stores. If you're

13

not skilled at making bows, use curling ribbon or raffia (ribbon made from natural fibers) to add a festive touch.

❑ Florist wire – This is not necessary, but is helpful for making and attaching bows. It can also be used to secure the cellophane or tulle around your gift basket.

Filler Items

The secret to keeping down the cost of your gift basket is to look for bargains when shopping for filler items. Check out these common sources for low-cost fillers.

❑ Dollar stores – Shop there for bath products, kitchen gadgets, coffee mugs, etc.

❑ Flea markets and garage sales – New and gently used books, household gizmos or cookbooks make great fillers.

❑ Consignment and thrift shops – Look for one-of-a-kind items such as unusual knickknacks and collectibles.

❑ Clearance tables – Practically every store has clearance merchandise. Look for great bargains on books, accessories or novelty items.

❑ Freebies – Trial sizes, samples and the extras you get when using buy one, get one free coupons are all fun fillers. Use a large group of them by themselves or add a handful of freebies to other gift basket items.

❑ Your own kitchen – What about homemade cookies and candies, flavored coffees or specialty breads? Used by themselves or in addition to other filler items, these goodies add a nice touch to any gift basket.

Endless Possibilities

Designing your gift basket is half the fun. To come up with something that is truly unique, think about the recipient's hobbies, interests or occupation and then create a basket that fits the person's unique personality. Here are a few examples.

❑ The aspiring chef – How about a basket of unusual spices, a cookbook, an apron and some recipe cards?

❑ The gardener – Include seed packets, gardening tools, work gloves and a book on gardening.

❑ The coffee lover – Give a basket containing a variety of flavored coffees, an attractive mug and some homemade biscotti.

❑ The home office worker – Give this person a basket of basic office supplies such as staples, paper clips, Post-It® Notes, CD-Rs (recordable discs), and a supply of ink pens.

❑ The college student living away from home – Put together a big basket of essentials such as laundry detergent, soap, shampoo, dish detergent, etc.

Putting It All Together

After you decide on a theme for your basket and have gathered all the filler items and supplies, the only thing left to do is put it all together. Although each personalized basket is unique, the basic steps for constructing all gift baskets are the same.

1. Start with a basket filled with filler material. Choose a basket in an appropriate size to accommodate the items you plan to put into it.

2. Arrange your filler items attractively in the basket. Put the largest items in first; fill in around the edges with the smaller items.

3. Wrap your basket, if you choose. Position your basket in the center of one or two large sheets of cellophane or tulle. Gather the cellophane or tulle tightly at the top of the basket and secure with tape or florist wire.

4. Attach a bow or ribbon. If you wrap your basket with cellophane or tulle, use a bow to cover the tape or florist wire. If you don't wrap it, attach the bow to the handle or along the rim on one side of the basket.

Gift baskets are easy for you to make and even easier for your friends and family members to love. What better way to give a personalized gift perfectly suited to the recipient's tastes?

Homemade Gift Ideas

If you are already well versed in the art of giving homemade gifts, I don't need to sell you on the benefits of this kind of giving. You already know that the process of expressing yourself by creating something unique is refreshing and fun. You know about the cost savings that you can usually enjoy when making presents yourself rather than purchasing them. And undoubtedly, you have already seen that in cases where the recipient could easily buy for herself anything she really wants or needs, giving a homemade gift is sometimes the only reasonable alternative.

> Making homemade gifts can be a major cause of holiday stress if not approached with moderation and realistic expectations.

As a side note, another benefit of making homemade gifts is that you can put your hobbies and special interests to good use by incorporating these skills into your gifting game plan. If you lead a busy life, you may feel guilty taking time to do something you love like knitting, candle making or woodworking. However, if you can multitask by making gifts and enjoying recreation at the same time, you will probably rest easier knowing that your playtime is also productive. If you don't already have a hobby that is useful for making gifts, consider taking a class or reading a book to help you learn a pleasurable pastime that you can also use in gift giving.

One point that should be noted, however, is that making homemade gifts can be a major cause of special occasion stress if not approached with moderation and realistic expectations. Remember my holiday horror story? Trying to give every person on my Christmas gift list—all twenty of them—several handmade items was just too lofty a goal, especially when my time for crafting was limited. Likewise, attempting to give a homemade gift for every gift giving occasion throughout the entire year may prove to be impractical.

Remember that giving handmade gifts is a means to an end for simplifying the way you celebrate special days. Making gifts just so you can take pride in the fact that you made them all yourself is a form of egotism. It's like boasting, "Hey, look what I can do!" On the other hand, creating gifts as a method of giving thoughtful gifts that are within your means is a worthy, honorable intention.

If you are new to the joys of making and giving homemade gifts or if you are simply looking for a few new gifts to give, here is a list of ideas to get you started.

Adult Gifts

- ❑ A personalized memory book or scrapbook filled with pictures, mementos and special memories from the recipient's life – This gift is delightful for any occasion but makes a particularly thoughtful gift for parents or grandparents on a milestone wedding anniversary.
- ❑ Gifts that are knitted or sewn by hand – If you can knit or crochet, why not make the honoree a new scarf, afghan or pair of mittens? If you sew, create a new apron, fleece throw or keepsake pillow.
- ❑ A family or office cookbook – Compile a cookbook with recipes contributed by all members. Or if people frequently ask for your recipes, make a cookbook of all your own special dishes to pass along to friends and relatives.
- ❑ Homemade scented candles or potpourri – Check out a book from the library on this or search the Internet for instructions.
- ❑ Homemade jams, jellies, relishes or pickles – Created with love in your own kitchen, these items make welcomed gifts.
- ❑ Homemade breads or candies – Give these in a decorative gift tin or a large brown paper bag that you decorated yourself.

- ❑ Gifts in a jar – Search the Internet for recipes for cookie, muffin and pancake mixes that you give in a jar. Include mixing and baking instructions so the recipient can enjoy the goodies later.
- ❑ Homemade flavored coffees, creamers and teas – These items make a wonderful gift all year round but are especially appreciated during the cold winter months.

Homemade Gifts for Kids and Teens

- ❑ A "Book about Me" – In an inexpensive journal, write a variety of statements on the blank pages such as, "When I grow up, I want to be..." or "What I like best about myself is...." Decorate the journal to fit the young person's tastes. If you like, include a new pen or mechanical pencil for the recipient to use when answering the questions.
- ❑ A personalized brag book – Fill a mini-photo album with photos of the child's friends, family and pets.
- ❑ Christmas ornaments – Why not start a tradition of giving the young person in your life a new ornament each year? When she moves away from home someday, she will have her own special collection of ornaments for her first Christmas tree.
- ❑ A personalized audio tape – Make a tape recording of yourself reading stories, singing songs, or reciting nursery rhymes that you know the child would enjoy.
- ❑ A personalized book for the recipient – Put your creative writing and artistic skills to work to create a book about the child's life or a make believe story starring the child. Add a tape recording of the story if the young person is not yet able to read.
- ❑ Homemade coupons or gift certificates – Make coupons redeemable for special privileges your young person would enjoy such as getting to stay up past her regular bedtime, a family movie night with her choice of movie rental and snacks, or an afternoon of window shopping at the local mall.

This list represents only a smattering of the endless possibilities. For more homemade gift ideas, check out the list of websites and helpful books about gift giving in Chapter Eleven: *Resources*.

Don't Get Wrapped on Gift Wrap

While on the topic of gifts, we shouldn't neglect the subject of wrapping and presenting your gift. If you're not careful, you can spend almost as much on gift wrap as you spend on the present itself. Presentation is important, but that doesn't mean it has to be expensive.

Here are some ideas for gift wrap that are not only inexpensive, but are also good for the environment. Remember that anytime you recycle and reuse something that would otherwise be thrown away, you do our planet a favor.

- ❑ Picture pages from decorative wall calendars
- ❑ Old maps, atlases or blueprints
- ❑ Pages of your children's artwork
- ❑ Colorful pages from junk mail catalogs
- ❑ Scraps of opaque fabric
- ❑ Decorative pillowcases – Tie the open end with ribbon.
- ❑ Old movie or celebrity posters
- ❑ Brown paper grocery bags decorated with markers, glitter, stickers or paint – Fold the top of the bag over to conceal the logo printed on the bag.
- ❑ Pages from an old phone book– You can also use this at the top of gift bags instead of plain tissue paper.
- ❑ Reusable containers such as tins, Tupperware® containers or canning jars – Just add a festive bow.
- ❑ Handmade cloth gift bags that can be reused each year
- ❑ The Sunday comics – The old and faithful standby for all-occasion gift wrap!

No matter how you choose to wrap your gift, don't let this aspect of the giving process get out of hand. Make sure that your method of gift wrapping is in keeping with your desire to give simple, yet meaningful tokens of your love.

~ *Part IV: Gifts of Time* ~

Sometimes when no other gift seems appropriate, the best possible offering you can give is the gift of yourself—specifically a sacrifice of your time. In the hustle-and-bustle society in which we live, our time is often more precious to us than our money. Like money, there never seems to be enough of it to go around. But unlike money that can be replaced if stolen or squandered, lost time is gone forever.

Giving the Gift of Your Time

The fact that most people are chronically busy is what makes a gift of your time so meaningful. First, it shows that you care enough to sacrifice one of your most valuable commodities. Many people would much rather give up some of their money than to sacrifice a portion of their precious free time. Additionally, it takes creativity to come up with a gift of time that the recipient will appreciate. Unlike store-bought presents, gifts of your time are not duplicable. Giving this type of gift also shows your practicality and sensitivity to the person's needs.

For those who have more time than cash, giving the gift of your time is a great way to show you care without overspending. These gifts are also ideal for recipients who seem to already have everything or could easily afford to buy anything they might want. Consider these questions as you brainstorm for ways to give the people on your gift list the present of your presence.

- ❑ Is there a time-consuming task you could offer to do that would give the recipient a welcomed break? How much fun is doing laundry, cleaning the house or cutting the grass each week? Who wouldn't love time off from these mundane but necessary duties?
- ❑ Is there a service for which the honoree usually pays that you could offer to perform as a gift? Help the recipient save money by offering to do home repairs, clean the carpets or change the oil in the car as your gift.
- ❑ Is there something the recipient needs to do but cannot do alone? Offer to help out with a task that seems too big for

one person such as cleaning the garage, landscaping or hanging wallpaper.

❑ Is there a way to combine your time and special talents to create a meaningful gift? If you are a great cook, create a special meal and then bring it to the recipients' house. Set the table, light the candles and then vamoose so they can enjoy a candlelit dinner for two. If you are skilled at organizing, offer to clean and organize that mess that is desperately in need of being conquered.

❑ What about your line of work? Could you provide free of charge a valuable service for which you would normally get paid? A professional mechanic could offer to do minor car repairs, while a massage therapist could give a relaxing massage treatment.

❑ Will the special occasion bring with it some special needs that you could meet? If the occasion is the birth of a baby, why not offer to keep the couple's other children during the delivery? Or how about cooking and freezing a week's worth of meals so the family can eat well while Mom is recovering?

❑ Would this person enjoy some uninterrupted, personalized attention? If the recipient doesn't drive, provide lunch and an afternoon of running errands as your gift. If the honoree is a young person, give the gift of a picnic and an afternoon of playing in the park.

How to Wrap the Gift of Your Time

From a practical standpoint, how do you actually give this kind of gift? As we established before, presentation is important. You don't want the recipient to feel that your gift of time was a hastily conjured gimmick you came up with because you didn't have time to buy a real gift! Here are a few of the many ways to make a memorable impression as you present your gift.

❑ Create a homemade gift certificate for the service or labor you plan to give using markers and construction paper or your computer's desktop publishing program. Enclose the certificate in a greeting card or creatively wrap it in a box as you would any other present.

❑ Write an IOU on fancy stationery and seal it in a matching envelope. For extra pizzazz, tape a small bow to the envelope.

❑ Give the recipient a small visual representation of your gift. For example, wrap up a new feather duster with an IOU for an afternoon of dusting and whatever other housecleaning she would like you to do.

❑ If your gift involves cooking, create a mock menu. List a variety of foods you are willing to make and ask the recipient to select the ones he would enjoy the most.

❑ If the task or service you plan to perform requires supplies you must purchase, wrap them up with a note explaining how you plan to use them. An example of this would be to place several packets of seeds in a gift bag. Include a note explaining that these will come in handy on the Saturday you spend helping the honoree plant a vegetable garden.

Chapter Two:
Simplifying the Christmas Celebration

"It's the most wonderful time of the year.
There'll be much mistletoeing
And hearts will be glowing,
When loved ones are near.
It's the most wonderful time of the year..."
            "It's The Most Wonderful Time of The Year"
            Eddie Pola and George Wyle

*A*ccording to this old song, the Christmas season is the most joyful and heartwarming time of the year. But is it really? For many people the words stressful and disappointing are more accurate descriptors. And what about "Peace on Earth, good will to men"? I have experienced many Yuletide seasons that were anything but peaceful and overflowing with good will. Haven't you?

~ Part I: Emotional Aspects of Christmas ~

Ironically, the very things that are supposed to bring joy to the season are often the source of tension. The giving and receiving of gifts is supposed to be pleasurable, but how can you experience this pleasure when you feel burdened with the pressure of finding the right gifts at reasonable prices in stores so crowded you can barely move? Likewise, good food and drink should enhance the merrymaking. Unfortunately, we often suffer the consequences of overindulgence because there is so much of this good food and drink available in such a short span of time. And the idea that Christmas is a time for family? This notion is hogwash if you don't have a family or if your family members can hardly stand to be in the same room with one another.

All of these conflicts and contradictions can make your Christmas season far from ideal. No wonder so many people suffer from holiday depression. Even if you aren't depressed, you may feel confused by anxiety over Christmas or a lack of enthusiasm over the season that is usually portrayed as magical and marvelous.

"Why Do I Feel This Way About Christmas?"

You'll notice as you read this book that I have a lot to say about Christmas. That is because the whole Christmas hubbub has always been rather unnerving for me. Even though our family has seen a brighter side of celebrating, each year it still takes a conscious effort on my part to drown out all the subtle messages of what Christmas should be. If I don't make this effort, I find myself disappointed because somehow the way things are supposed to be never quite matches the way they really are.

I have to remind myself that this concept of a perfect holiday—one where every gathering is flawless and each gift I give registers a 10 on the recipient's "wow-o-meter"—is a societal myth. If I judge the success of my family's Christmas celebration against an unrealistic image of perfection, my family's celebration will undoubtedly fall short every time.

In times past, before I made this realization, I always experienced dismay and dissatisfaction over the Yuletide season. Each year after the last ornament was packed away and all the leftovers were gone, I found myself feeling empty. "Where was all the meaning? Where was all the magic," I would think. "And why did I feel so *blah* when I was supposed to be brimming with Christmas joy?"

Maybe you are shaking your head in agreement right now. You, too, may have experienced this feeling of holiday letdown. Or for you, it may have come in the form of ambivalence or downright antagonism toward the holiday season. Whatever the feelings, I believe the culprit is what I call "Christmas overload." Somewhere around September or October, retailers begin peddling Christmas joy and don't let up until after New Year's Day. Everywhere we look, we're surrounded by this artificial,

24

commercialized brand of Christmas spirit. No wonder so many of us feel let down when Christmas day finally comes and goes without the big bang you'd expect after three months of hype.

Christmas overload is like eating your favorite food at every meal for three months straight. Even your favorite dish would become sickening when eaten to such excess. The same is true with Christmas. How can we truly enjoy something that has been forced down our throats for months? Remember that old expression, "Familiarity breeds contempt"?

I don't want to sound as though I am anti-Christmas or that having a good holiday season is not important to me. In the years since we've been married, Michael and I have learned to fine-tune our Christmas celebration so that it is more like what we really want rather than what we know we don't want. Believe me, this education wasn't an accident. It took a few holidays filled with frazzled nerves, short tempers and way too much stress to help us to see the light. Out of a desperate determination not to repeat these miserable performances, we knew we had to do things differently to avoid Christmas overload in the future.

> If you judge the success of your family's Christmas celebration against an unrealistic image of perfection, your family's celebration will undoubtedly fall short.

Cultural Challenges with Christmas

If ever there was a Christmas machine that needed to be unplugged, it was certainly running willy-nilly at my house the year I did my infamous Grinch impersonation. Soon after that holiday fiasco, I marched myself down to the nearest library. I knew I had to find something—anything that would help me learn how to do things differently the next year.

That's when I stumbled across Jo Robinson and Jean Coppock Staeheli's book, *Unplug the Christmas Machine: A Complete Guide to Putting Love and Joy Back into the Season* (Quill, 1991). I believe this book should be required reading for everyone who wants to simplify her family's Christmas celebration. The insights the authors share in this book were of great help to me in realizing where I had gone wrong in my efforts to orchestrate a larger-than-life Christmas celebration.

The book starts by examining the traditional roles men and women play in the Christmas celebration and how these roles cause problems. According to Robinson and Staeheli, women typically are the Christmas Magicians. "Like their mothers before them, women are responsible for transforming their family's everyday lives into a beautiful, magical festival." This added responsibility, along with all the other duties women fulfill, often pushes the level of stress beyond toleration.

> The same old actions bring about the same old results every year unless you make a conscious effort to create a celebration that reflects your desire for a meaningful holiday season.

If women are the Christmas Magicians, the authors explain, then men are the Christmas Stagehands: "Like their fathers before them, men expect to play a subordinate part in the celebration." Although many men are happy to let their wives take charge, they often find that being so uninvolved is a major source of their dissatisfaction with the holiday. And what about the role of children? The authors state that children are one of the prime targets of the Christmas Machine because toys make up such a large, dependable portion of holiday retail sales. Unless parents work hard to teach their children otherwise, children quickly come to believe that opening presents is all there is to Christmas.

Unplug the Christmas Machine helped me to further understand that the cultural norms in our society for Christmas celebrations are inherently flawed. The way things have always been done set the stage for the very trappings most of us wish to avoid. Thus, having a different kind of celebration requires doing something different. The same old actions bring about the same old results every year unless we make a conscious effort to create a celebration reflective of our desire for a meaningful holiday season.

Keeping Your Eye on the Goal

Although Michael and I have learned a great deal about creating meaningful family celebrations, we have also discovered that we must constantly be on guard. We have seen how easy it is to get off track if we don't stay focused on celebrating in ways that reflect our values. Just a few years ago, I received a humbling reminder of what the meaning of Christmas should be for me.

Our backyard had no landscaping when we purchased our house. The only vegetation we had was a sparse layer of grass with a pitiful collection of young pine trees. Being a man of vision, my husband quickly dubbed this group of trees our Christmas tree farm soon after we moved in. With all of those fine specimens of Christmas trees growing on our property, he wouldn't hear of actually purchasing one the first holiday season we lived here. He insisted we had to cut our Christmas tree from our own backyard.

On tree-cutting day that year, we selected and cut down the least spindly tree of the bunch. It wasn't exactly the Christmas tree of my dreams and I confess that I made a point of loudly telling Michael so several times. In fact, I think he may have been a little hurt and disappointed that I didn't seem impressed by his resourcefulness.

Anyway, the lesson for me came later as my conscience bothered me for not showing more gratitude over our less-than-perfect, yet free, Christmas tree. I was reminded once again that the reason for the Christmas season is not outward displays of seasonal merriment, but rather inward reflection and the celebration of what you hold most dear.

As a Christian, the wonder of the Christmas season for me is that a perfect little baby was born into a far-from-perfect world so that "ugly Christmas trees" everywhere could become beautiful through God's love. In the same way our lights and decorations covered our little tree's imperfections, God's grace and forgiveness make those who accept Him whole and complete and perfect in His sight. As God showed His love for us, we show our love to those around us during this season of giving.

> The bottom line is simple: What do you really want out of your celebration and what do you need to do to see that you and your family get it?

When I thought about it that way, our ugly Christmas tree didn't look so bad after all. In fact, being quite a bit less than perfect myself, I could even empathize with the little tree. Thank goodness God doesn't look for the same perfection in us that I was looking for in a Christmas tree! And thank goodness holiday success is not a reflection of how attractive your decorations are or how many presents surround the base of your tree.

This little story illustrates that simplifying the holidays is a continual process of defining and redefining what a meaningful celebration is for you. This principle is true for Christmas and it holds true for other holidays as well. Forget about how you believe everyone else celebrates. The bottom line is simple: What do you really want out of your celebration, and what do you need to do to see that you and your family get it?

Finding Christmas Joy When You Don't Feel Joyful

Have you ever wished you could bypass the December holiday season altogether? Maybe illnesses, financial struggles or family conflicts throughout the year drained you emotionally, leaving you with little energy or desire to participate in holiday rituals. One of the most stubborn Christmas myths is the idea that no matter what difficulties or challenges a person faces during the other eleven months of the year, somehow seasonal joy will automatically kick in around December 1st.

If you have ever wondered how you could muster up Christmas joy, you aren't alone. One Christmas after a particularly difficult year, I actually said to Michael, "I wish Christmas would just go away!" Could any sentiment possibly sound less joyful than that? I made the comment while Michael and I discussed whether or not we should get a Christmas tree that year. With finances being fairly tight, we both knew that even $15-20 for a small tree was more than we should spend. After all, Christmas trees don't exactly fall into the category of necessary expenses. (In case you're wondering, after sap dripped all over the carpet and we found creepy crawlies everywhere, Michael decided that cutting a Christmas tree from the pines out back wasn't as good an idea as he originally thought!)

I knew we should save our money that year, yet I wondered how I could possibly get in the Christmas spirit without a tree. I felt depressed and even a little deprived. And having such a small budget for presents made me wonder how Christmas could possibly be merry when we had so little to give.

Intellectually, I knew Christmas is not about what kind of tree you have or how much you spend on presents, but emotionally I needed a reminder. Thankfully, I got that reminder just a few days later. It came as I was thinking about the decorations we have and what I could come up with to substitute for a tree. Then I remembered our Joy ornament. The first year we were married, Michael and I made a Christmas ornament that we've used ever since. From thin plywood, Michael cut out the shape of the word JOY approximately a foot wide by eight inches tall. I painted it beige and outlined the letters in gold. During our first few Christmases, we used it to decorate our mantel. Later, we always attached it near the top of our Christmas tree, just below our cornhusk angel tree topper.

At the time we made the ornament, I didn't give much thought to its meaning. But that particular year, as I dreaded celebrating the holiday without a large tree and lots of presents, I realized that the Joy ornament could teach me a lesson about true Christmas joy if I'd only let it.

As a child, I was taught that the letters in J-O-Y stood for Jesus first, Others second, Yourself last. If you want to be happy, I learned, you have to keep your priorities in that order. If you ever get them mixed up, you won't have true joy. When I thought about it, this simple equation seemed like the perfect way to find Christmas joy even though my initial attitude toward the season was anything but joyful.

> At times when you don't feel like celebrating, experiencing Christmas joy is easier than you think when you keep your priorities in perspective.

If you have ever had trouble getting into the Christmas spirit for whatever reason, let me share with you how I put the J-O-Y principle to work. Putting Jesus first, I committed myself to celebrating Jesus' birthday in a way that would be pleasing to Him. He didn't come into the world with a lot of meaningless hoopla so I don't think He would want me to celebrate that way, either. Instead, I was sure He'd want me to celebrate with the very things that are so hard to give during the busy season. In the weeks before Christmas, I looked for ways to give Him quiet reflection, purposeful introspection, and wholehearted appreciation.

To put others second, I made a commitment to find creative ways to give of myself while still giving within my means. As I cooked up and crafted homemade gifts for family members and friends, I tried to add little extra touches to make each gift special for the recipient. Instead of feeling badly that I couldn't buy expensive gifts, I focused on using my time and talents to express my love.

Putting myself last meant forgetting any preconceived notions of what tangible holiday traditions were necessary for my family to have a good Christmas. I knew that if I busied myself enough with the first two objectives, there wouldn't be much time left to worry about feeling sorry for myself.

This plan worked well. Instead of wishing the holidays would go away, I soon found myself looking forward to Christmas. At times when you find the thought of holiday happiness and good cheer repulsive, I encourage you to try the J-O-Y principle. You will most likely find, as I did, that experiencing Christmas joy is easier than you think when you keep your priorities in perspective.

Learning From Your Christmas Mistakes

Earlier I shared my story of a horribly out-of-control holiday. To say that particular Christmas wasn't very merry would be an understatement. With all the frantic flurry of activity surrounding the making and giving of presents, celebrating the holiday in a meaningful way quickly got lost in the shuffle. How could I possibly find time to attend a Christmas cantata or volunteer at a homeless shelter when there was so much to do and so little time left before Present Day?

Actually, a few good things did come out of my major Christmas catastrophe. Besides my motivation to write this book, the whole ordeal helped me to see the danger of allowing myself to lose focus. That particular holiday season was doomed from day one because I strayed so far from the simplicity I value in holiday celebrations.

From this regretful experience, I also walked away with fierce determination not to let it happen again. Had I not ever seen how awful and ugly the out-of-control holiday monster can be, I would not feel so strongly about keeping that monster in its place—far, far away from my family's holiday celebrations.

In a final twist of irony, I received a more realistic view of my own ability to give without expecting anything in return. One aspect of my horrible holiday that I haven't shared yet is that in addition to making homemade gifts for all my family members and friends, I also cooked up platters of homemade treats for everyone in my office. For each of my supervisors with whom I worked closely, I made an individual gift basket of homemade flavored coffees complete with chocolate-dipped spoons for stirring.

On the big day that I brought all the goodies to work and distributed them, something curious happened. Of all the people I had tried so hard to impress with my wonderful culinary creations, only two reciprocated in any way. Sure, the others thanked me for my gifts, but somehow their thanks didn't seem as enthusiastic as I'd hoped. No one did back flips; no one danced a jig. No one said, "Gee, you're the greatest!"

> Do you have your own share of holiday mishaps and missteps you'd rather forget? Before you forget them, try to learn from your mistakes.

As I felt rather awkward and uncomfortable over the situation, I realized that my motives in trying to wow everyone with extravagant homemade delicacies were not altogether pure. If they had been, why would I feel unappreciated and overlooked when the recipients didn't respond with thunderous rounds of applause? Apparently, my giving had not been the selfless, altruistic variety I imagined.

The truth was that somewhere in the deep recesses of my mind, I felt that even if others didn't reciprocate with gifts, they at least owed me a heartfelt thank you. So much for giving without expecting anything in return! I am embarrassed to admit I could have possibly felt this way, but at least I walked away from that experience with a clearer picture of my own weaknesses. I also learned how easily pride and unrealistic expectations can invade my gift giving.

Do you have your own share of holiday mishaps and missteps you'd rather forget? Before you forget them, I encourage you to learn, as I did, from your mistakes. Spend some time thinking about what went wrong and what you did to contribute to the blunder. Did you ignore your inner voice of reason in setting and sticking to spending limits? Did you let meal planning and preparation get out of hand? Did senseless procrastination cause stress to skyrocket? Whatever you could have done differently, don't berate yourself for your contribution to the situation. Instead make a commitment to yourself that you will do things differently next time. If you need accountability in keeping your promise, make the commitment to your family members as well so they can help you stick to it.

~ *Part II: Logistical Aspects of Christmas* ~

Christmas Overload: Do You Suffer From It?

Earlier we discussed what I call Christmas overload—anxiety, ambivalence or even antagonism toward the holiday season caused in part from too much Christmas commercialism being forced upon you from the months of October through December. This commercialism is not the only cause, however. Let's take a minute to look at some other causes and symptoms. Read through this list and see if any of these ring particularly true for you.

❑ Feeling pressured to spend more than you can afford on gifts, food and entertaining

❑ Trying to participate in too many activities within too short a period of time

❑ Trying to fulfill unrealistic expectations, either your own or those of others

❑ Feeling obligated to participate in activities or family rituals you'd rather avoid

❑ Trying to attain holiday perfection, especially when your concept of what makes a holiday memorable is vague

❑ Taking personal responsibility for others' holiday happiness

❑ Not taking appropriate action to change a predictably unpleasant holiday scenario

❑ Unhappiness over the discrepancy between how you actually celebrate and how you truly want to celebrate the holiday

In addition to these causes, here are some humorous and some not-so-humorous symptoms that indicate you suffer from this holiday malady.

❑ The very thought of Christmas gives you cold sweats.

❑ It takes you six months to recover financially from Christmas.

34

- ❏ The idea of sleeping through the whole month of December sounds appealing.
- ❏ The stress of Christmas ranks right up there with getting a root canal and having your pipes burst.
- ❏ Unlike your children who count the days until Christmas comes, you count down the days until it is over.
- ❏ Your nickname is "Grinch," "Scrooge" or "Ebenezer."
- ❏ Your dog and cat get more excited about the holiday than you do.
- ❏ Every year when it's all over, you realize that the true meaning got lost in the shuffle again.

Combating Christmas Overload

What if after careful evaluation of the causes and symptoms above, you see that you and your family are victims of Christmas overload? Something needs to change, you're convinced, but you don't know exactly what or how to go about making those changes.

First, I applaud you for recognizing that you want something better than the run-of-the-mill celebration. So many people have a vague sense of dissatisfaction over the way their families celebrate, but they don't take the time to examine this uneasiness and its source. Your recognition that things could be better is a positive step in the right direction. Here are a few of the tactics we used the year after our disastrous holiday season to ensure that the next Yuletide season was not more of the same.

Scale Back. First, we scaled back our gift giving considerably. Trying to give handmade gifts to all the friends, family members and coworkers on our list was just too lofty a goal. Do you also have some tradition that has become too much to handle? Maybe you cook Christmas dinner for your large family or make homemade candy for the whole neighborhood. Whatever it is, try scaling back to a more manageable proportion. Look for ways to show you care without overextending yourself.

Start Early. Next, we started Christmas shopping early so we were almost finished by Thanksgiving. We did most of our

Christmas shopping by purchasing new and like-new gift items at summer yard sales. Not only did we save money, but we also avoided the holiday rush. Are there other things you could also do in advance? Why wait until the last minute? Completing as many tasks in advance as possible eases the stress of the busy holiday season.

Plan Meaningful Activities. Because we started early and scaled back, we found that we had more free time during the holidays. For once, we actually had time to do things like visit a nursing home and deliver gifts to needy families. These activities brought meaning to our holiday season. What kind of activities would enrich the holidays for you? Plan several weeks or even months ahead of time for volunteer or charitable activities you want to include. If you don't plan in advance, most likely you won't find time for them at the last minute.

Say "No" Sometimes. By nature, I find it difficult to say no. The year after our very un-merry Christmas, Michael made it his job to help me set boundaries when our schedule began to fill. Do you have trouble with the N word? Don't feel you have to do everything. If necessary, enlist the support of your spouse or an objective friend who can help you determine which activities to keep and which need to get the ax.

Proactive Simplification

Because Michael and I wanted a different kind of celebration, we knew we had to do something different. Sounds elementary, doesn't it? But too many times, we fail to see this simple truth.

Do you wish every year for a less stressful holiday season? This year, don't just dream about a simpler Christmas. Make it a reality by taking action. Consider these positive steps you can take in the months before the holiday season—September, October, November or even earlier—to set the stage for a less hectic, more enjoyable celebration in December.

❑ If you follow the advice in Chapter One: *Meaningful Gift Giving* about starting a gift shelf, you will probably have most of your Christmas shopping done long before September. But if not, don't wait until the stores are crowded with thousands of holiday shoppers. In the months prior to the traditional shopping season, elicit Christmas wish lists from family members and get going.

❑ Take care of time-consuming tasks. Writing Christmas cards, wrapping gifts, boxing up presents to mail—why wait until December to attend to these time-consuming details? Knock them out now.

❑ Fill your freezer. Each time you cook, double your recipes and freeze the extra portions, or do once-a-month cooking. See the Christmas section in Chapter Eleven: *Resources* for books on the topic of cooking in bulk. During the hectic weeks before Christmas, having meals in the freezer will be a lifesaver.

❑ Plan volunteer activities now. Does your intention of doing some kind of community service always seem to get lost in the holiday shuffle each year? Schedule these activities now so they won't get overlooked when things get busy. Use the months prior to the holidays to investigate various opportunities for service and decide which one you want to include in your Christmas season.

❑ Complete Christmas crafts. If you plan to give any handcrafted gifts, plan to have them finished by Thanksgiving, or better yet, Halloween. Work a few hours each weekend until you're done.

❑ Plan holiday meals. Write out menus and shopping lists for dinners and get-togethers so you won't have to think about it later. Also use this time to experiment with any new recipes you plan to use.

❑ Decide what to delete. Which obligations add to your stress level each year? What activities would you rather forgo? Decide in advance how to diplomatically decline these engagements.

If your life is constantly running at high speed, you may feel overwhelmed when you read this list of ways to proactively simplify Christmas. You may barely have time to complete the things you have to do each day, much less perform tasks for a holiday several months away. If you are in that predicament, let me encourage you to take things one step at a time. Many of the tasks above can be done while you're doing something you would normally do anyway. Try to incorporate a little advance preparation into your normal routines.

Your family has to eat every day, right? Why not double your recipes and put the extra portion in the freezer to save for use in December? Use the time you spend in front of the television each week for wrapping gifts, addressing Christmas cards or working on crafts. And don't forget to include a little Christmas shopping as you run your normal errands. Proactive simplification is manageable when you do a little at a time and combine Christmas preparations with tasks you must do anyway.

Getting Your Gifting Done Early

Completing all your Christmas preparations in advance is desirable, but for some, it may not be possible. If you can only manage one positive step toward Christmas simplification, I suggest you do yourself a favor by taking care of gift making and buying in advance. Even if you can't do anything else to simplify your celebration, this one accomplishment will relieve a great deal of stress during your holiday season.

In addition to stress reduction, another huge benefit of getting your gifting done early is that you can take advantage of sales and special savings opportunities as you encounter them. You don't have to make buying decisions under pressure, but can take your time to find suitable gifts at prices you can afford. This step also reduces the stress that holiday gift giving puts on your budget because you do your shopping throughout the year rather than purchasing everything within the last few weeks before Christmas.

Here is the simplest way I know to accomplish this. First, make a list of everyone on your Christmas list. Write down what you plan to give each person. If you're not sure yet, write down ideas for gifts you think each person would enjoy. Keep the list handy as you go about your normal errands and activities. Be on the lookout for inexpensive gift items in such places as:

- ❏ Clearance sales and sidewalk sales
- ❏ Sales by online vendors and mail order catalogs
- ❏ Craft fairs
- ❏ Going out of business sales
- ❏ Flea markets
- ❏ School fundraisers
- ❏ Garage sales (for brand-new and like-new gift items)

Likewise, if you plan to make Christmas gifts, keep your eyes open for food and craft items you can make and give as gifts. Ideas are everywhere. You just have to be prepared to recognize a good idea when you see it. By starting early, you can also take time to do Internet searches and ask friends to share their handmade gift ideas. After you find some ideas that suit your fancy, take a few hours each week to work on your crafts, rather than cramming them all into the few weeks between Thanksgiving and Christmas. Even if you plan to give edible homemade gifts that cannot be made too far in advance, you can at least do the work of deciding what you'll make and gathering supplies and nonperishable ingredients.

Meaningful Holiday Activities

One of the most insidious causes of Christmas overload is the cramming of too many activities into a relatively short a period of time. To make matters worse, the number of holiday activities is multiplied by the number of people in your family. Even small children contribute with their share of Christmas pageants, parties and get-togethers to the list of outings Mom and Dad feel compelled to attend.

Everyone would agree that the holidays are overly busy. One of the steps Michael and I have taken over the years to simplify our Christmas celebration is to plan meaningful activities. At first consideration this may sound ludicrous. Why would you want to add even more activity to an already hectic season? Rather than more activity, we focus on fewer activities that have been carefully screened to add the maximum value and significance to the season.

The key to incorporating meaningful activities into your holiday season is to look for opportunities in which the whole family can participate together. Seek out avenues that focus on serving others and celebrating the spiritual aspects of the holiday. Here is a list of activity ideas to consider.

- ❏ Schedule some family devotional time for rereading the biblical account of the Christmas story and singing Christmas hymns. Let family members take turns reading or choosing songs to sing.
- ❏ Spend an afternoon with the kids making homemade Christmas cookies and cards for the elderly people in your church or neighbors who may be especially lonely during the holidays.
- ❏ Since Christmas is a celebration of Jesus' birth, plan a birthday party complete with cake, candles and the "Happy Birthday" song. Family members can even use craft supplies to make visual representations of gifts they want to offer Jesus during the upcoming year such as a forgiving heart or hands that help others.
- ❏ Make a trip to the local nursing home or children's hospital for caroling, handing out homemade Christmas cookies, giving small gifts or just visiting with residents and patients.
- ❏ Spend an afternoon looking through old family pictures of Christmases past. Take turns with other family members sharing favorite holiday memories.
- ❏ Grandparents who live near their grandchildren can plan a special kids-only time for enjoying food and fellowship. In addition to giving the children some special time alone with Grandma and Grandpa, this activity also provides a wonderful opportunity for parents to enjoy time alone.
- ❏ Practice random acts of kindness as a family. Look for ways you can anonymously fulfill a need or do a good deed for someone who needs encouragement.
- ❏ Rather than purchasing a precut tree, take your family to a Christmas tree farm and cut your own. Later on, as you

decorate the tree, reminisce how each unique ornament came into the family collection.

❑ Watch the newspaper for free church plays and musicals that depict the story of Christ's birth.

❑ Volunteer to help serve a holiday meal at the local homeless shelter. If a holiday meal is not being served, ask how you can help out in another way.

In adding activities to your family's Christmas schedule, try to swap one or two events that are less meaningful for each new activity you add. Remember also to be flexible. If a particular outing doesn't go as well as you would like one year, try something else the next year.

~ *Part III: Spiritual Aspects of Christmas* ~

I believe that intellectually all Christians know the reason for the Christmas season. Ironically, there is little evidence of spiritual significance in the way many of us celebrate. Often, Santa Claus plays a bigger role in the festivities than Jesus. Sadly, the Good News of Christ's birth is given only a cursory nod before moving on to what has become the *real* reason for Christmas—receiving a windfall of goodies from the jolly fellow in the red suit.

Adding Spiritual Significance to Your Christmas Celebration

For years I knew something wasn't right about the way our family celebrated Christmas, but not until recent years did I realize what was wrong. After giving it much thought, I found that a major source of my discontentment with the Yuletide holidays was the lack of spiritual meaning that our celebrations contained.

I grew up in a Christian home, yet Christmas was not really celebrated as a spiritual holiday. Because the Bible does not specifically tell us when Jesus was born, the church group to which we belonged was very leery of putting too much emphasis on Christmas as a celebration of Christ's birth. In the weeks prior to December 25th, our church sang a few Christmas hymns and the preacher always delivered some kind of Christmas sermon. At home, we decorated our tree, opened presents on Christmas Eve and enjoyed a large meal on Christmas Day. That was the extent of Christmas as I knew it.

When Michael and I were married, we brought into our marriage similar backgrounds of Christmas celebrations. Neither of us grew up celebrating Christmas as a spiritual holiday, so we didn't know how to begin doing so as we started our own family traditions. After several less than fulfilling Christmas seasons, we began exploring ways to make Christ the center of our celebrations. With each passing year, we continue to learn more about celebrating in ways that express the faith we hold dear.

Broadening Your Holiday Horizons

One way to put Christ back into your Christmas holidays is to extend your family's celebration to include Advent and Epiphany. The Advent season includes the weeks prior to Christmas Day; it is a celebration of the anticipation that preceded the coming of Christ. Epiphany occurs after Christmas and is a commemoration of the arrival of the Wise Men to worship the Christ child. If you grew up in a faith that follows the Church Calendar, you are probably very familiar with the benefits of including these special days in your Christmas season.

Celebrating Advent is a wonderful way to counteract the rampant commercialism that permeates the month of December. Each traditional symbol and activity offers an opportunity to redirect the focus of the season to spiritual matters. Each of the Advent traditions can be done at home and provide educational opportunities for the whole family. Having something special to do each day or week makes Christmas more than just a one-day gift and food orgy. Often both children and adults experience letdown after the presents are opened because it

> Sadly, the Good News of Christ's birth is often given only a cursory nod before moving on to what has become the *real* reason for Christmas—receiving a windfall of presents from the jolly fellow in the red suit.

seems there is nothing left to celebrate. Because Epiphany occurs a few weeks after Christmas, this observance gives family members something else to look forward to.

When you think about it, how can something as monumental to the Christian faith as the birth of Jesus truly receive the recognition it deserves in only one day? Celebrating the days of

Advent offers a way to spread out the festivities and build up excitement. Likewise, something so exceptional shouldn't end abruptly at 11:59 p.m. on December 25th. Extending the holidays to include Epiphany reminds us that the joy of Christ's birth is something we should carry with us all year long.

A Bit of Background Information

> When you think about it, how can something as monumental to the Christian faith as the birth of Jesus truly receive the recognition it deserves in only one day?

Before we discuss ways your family can observe Advent and Epiphany, let's take a minute to talk about the Church Calendar— what it is and how it came to be. In the Old Testament, God required the Israelites to observe a regular schedule or calendar of feasts and festivals. As Christianity replaced Judaism in the New Testament, early Christians did not observe Jewish holidays anymore, but instead only celebrated each Sunday as a commemoration of Jesus' Resurrection.

Over time, the Church formed its own schedule of special observances, which is still followed by many denominations today. The purpose of this Church Calendar is to teach Christians lessons about their faith throughout the entire year. The two primary celebrations are commemorations of the most basic tenets of the Christian faith: God becoming flesh and living among us (Christmas) and Jesus dying for our sins and resurrecting from the dead (Easter). All other holidays on the Church Calendar revolve around these two celebrations and the lessons they teach. The Church Calendar consists of two parts. The seasons in the first half of the calendar focus on what God did for man, while the seasons in the second half focus on man's response to God.

Rather than beginning on January 1st, the Church Calendar begins with Advent. This season begins four Sundays prior to Christmas Day and is a time of preparation for the observance of Christ's birth. The celebration of Epiphany occurs 12 days after Christmas. Next comes the season of Lent, which includes the 40 days before Easter (excluding Sundays) and prepares Christians for the celebration of the Resurrection. After Easter, the season of Pentecost is celebrated. Beginning the 50th day after Easter and continuing until the day before Advent, this season is a time for Christians to focus on how they respond personally to God's love shown through Jesus' birth and resurrection.

Creating Your Own Family Advent Celebration

Advent is a time of preparation. The word Advent means coming, and it is a time to prepare yourself to celebrate the coming of Jesus as the Messiah. It is a time of waiting and anticipation, a time for readying yourself through repentance and the study of biblical promises regarding the Savior.

A variety of traditions have evolved to help draw families into this season of preparation. As you read the following descriptions of various Advent traditions, think about how you could implement some of these activities into your family's Christmas celebrations. There is no rule that says you have to implement them all, and you don't have to implement the activities you choose all at once. If celebrating Advent is new to you, why not choose one new Advent tradition this year to add spiritual significance to your family celebration? You can always add other activities later.

The Advent Wreath

The Advent wreath is probably the most familiar Advent tradition. The wreath is usually a circle of greenery containing four or five candles. The exact colors of the candles and order in which they are lighted varies, but typically three of the candles are purple to represent both the royalty of Christ as King and also our penitence for our sins. These are the Hope, Love and Peace candles. These candles are lighted to remind us of the hope we have in Christ, the love God showed in sending His

45

Son, and the peace that comes through knowing Jesus as our Savior. The fourth candle is the Joy candle. It is pink or rose-colored and reminds us of the joy of Jesus' coming. If five candles are used, the fifth one is the Christ candle and it is white to represent His purity.

On each of the four Sundays during Advent, a new candle in the wreath is lighted along with any candles that were lighted on previous Sundays. If five candles are used, the fifth candle is lighted on Christmas Eve or Christmas Day. With each passing Sunday, the volume of light produced by the burning candles increases. The bright light of all candles aglow on the last day represents the fulfillment of Jesus coming to be the Light of the world.

The lighting of the Advent candles each week can be the springboard for times of family devotions. Get children involved by allowing one sibling to light the candles while another reads passages of scripture about the coming Messiah. If you want, sing a Christmas hymn and say a short prayer together. For maximum effectiveness, remember to keep this time short so you won't lose family members' attention. For information and ideas on Advent devotions, see the Christmas section in Chapter Eleven: *Resources*.

Another way to involve the kids is to let them make the family Advent wreath. Your wreath does not have to be made of greenery. It can also be made of bread or even Play-Doh®. To make a bread wreath, divide a batch of bread dough into three parts. Roll each part into a long strand. Braid the three strands and then connect the ends of the braid to make a circular wreath shape. Before baking until golden brown, press the end of your Advent candles down into the dough to create a place for each candle to lodge. To make a Play-Doh® wreath, use enough green dough to make a large ring. Press the ends of the candles down into the clay to make a place for the candles to go. After the dough air-dries and hardens, use a hot glue gun to attach greenery, nuts, small pinecones and whatever other decorations you choose.

The Advent Calendar

Another popular tradition is the Advent calendar, which provides a fun daily reminder of the meaning of the Christmas holiday. Usually the calendar is a large piece of cardboard or poster board with one flap for each day from the first Sunday of Advent until Christmas Day. Under each flap is a scripture verse or suggested activity. Family members open only one flap each day as they count down the days until Christmas.

Advent calendars can be purchased commercially and come in all varieties. An easy way to make your own is to start with a large piece of felt or poster board. Cut small rectangles of felt, cloth or construction paper, one for each of the days in the Advent season. Because the actual number of days in the Advent season varies from year to year, you may want to start your Advent calendar at December 1st so you can use it for many years.

Arrange the rectangles in rows on the large piece of felt or poster board. Using white glue or a hot glue gun, attach three sides of each small rectangle to the large piece to form a pocket. Use fabric paint or markers to number each pocket. Decorate the rest of your Advent calendar any way you wish. In each pocket place a slip of paper containing a scripture or an act of kindness to be done that day (e.g., Make holiday cookies and share them with your neighbors today.) To make the Advent calendar even more fun for the kids, add small candy canes or other surprises to each pocket. Take time each day as a family to read and talk about that day's note.

The Chrismon Tree

Chrismons are Christian symbols used to decorate a Christmas tree. The name, Chrismon, is a contraction of "Christ monograms." These ornaments help convey the story of Christ through symbols. Often churches choose to decorate their holiday trees with handmade Chrismons because of their spiritual significance rather than using traditional ornaments that hold no meaning.

Chrismons are typically gold and white. Gold represents the majesty of Jesus as King and white represents His purity and perfection. If any lights are used along with the Chrismons to decorate the tree, they are always white as well. The Chrismons remind us of events in the life of Jesus and also biblical promises regarding the Savior. Some are Old Testament symbols; others are symbols from the early days of Christianity. Common symbols include a crown of thorns, an Ichthus (Christian fish), a cross, the Star of David, a manger, a lamb and the Greek letters Alpha and Omega.

Chrismon trees are usually used in churches, but can also be used in the home as a wonderful teaching tool to help family members learn more about Jesus' life and ministry on earth. Your family may choose to decorate your Christmas tree entirely with Chrismons or use them in conjunction with other decorations. Another idea is to use a small tabletop tree to create your own family Chrismon Tree. All family members can contribute by making special Chrismon ornaments for the tree. For information and ideas on making Chrismons, visit the websites listed under Christmas Resources in Chapter Eleven: *Resources*.

The Jesse Tree

One last Advent tradition that we should mention is the Jesse Tree. This special tree is very similar to the Chrismon tree, except the symbols represent biblical characters in the lineage of Jesus. The symbols can also represent Old Testament events that demonstrate God's love toward man. The Jesse Tree gets its name from the prophecy found in Isaiah 11:1 which says, "A shoot will come up from the stump of Jesse; from his roots a Branch will bear fruit." Common symbols include Noah's ark, David's harp, Jacob's ladder and stone tablets like the ones that bore the Ten Commandments.

The beauty of the Jesse Tree is that it provides an extraordinary opportunity to educate children about the Old Testament and the many years of waiting for the Messiah to come. Just as God's people had to wait patiently for the fulfillment of His promises, family members must also wait for Christmas day to arrive. The symbols also serve as reminders of God's faithfulness throughout history.

Some Jesse Trees are made from a branch of a tree secured in some kind of pot. However, a small tabletop tree or even a tree cut from poster board or construction paper can be used in creating your own Jesse Tree. Allow your children to use their creativity and artistic abilities in making the symbolic ornaments to decorate the tree. One ornament can be added each day during the Advent season or add several ornaments on each of the four Sundays preceding Christmas. As ornaments are placed on the Jesse Tree, spend time discussing the story behind each symbol and how the person or event relates to the coming of Jesus. For ideas and information on making a Jesse Tree, visit the websites listed in the Christmas section in Chapter Eleven: *Resources*.

> Celebrating Epiphany is a wonderful conclusion to a season honoring God's gift of love to mankind.

Including Epiphany in Your Holiday Celebration

In Matthew's account of the birth of Jesus, we are told that Magi or Wise Men from the East followed a guiding star to Bethlehem. The Bible says that there they found Joseph, Mary and Jesus in a house. This indicates their visit did not occur on the night of Jesus' birth, but probably as much as two years later. When the Wise Men found the Child, they worshiped Him and presented Him with the finest of gifts. Because the Bible records three gifts that were given—gold, frankincense and myrrh—tradition has it that there were three wise men who came to worship. Also, because the gifts were of such an expensive nature, it is believed that the men must have been royalty. For these reasons, the Magi are often referred to as the Three Kings.

Epiphany commemorates the arrival of the Wise Men to pay homage to the new King. The word Epiphany means manifestation; this holiday reminds us that God showed Himself to us in the form of His Son, Jesus. Because the Magi were not

Jewish, this occasion also commemorates God's love and salvation for all people, Jews as well as Gentiles.

The period between Christmas and Epiphany has been called the original 12 days of Christmas. In some cultures, Christians do not exchange gifts on Christmas because it is celebrated strictly as a spiritual holiday. Instead, they wait until Epiphany and give gifts then to imitate the gifts that the Wise Men gave to the Christ Child.

Celebrated on January 6th, this special holiday is a wonderful conclusion to a season honoring God's gift of love to mankind. If you'd like to extend your family's Christmas celebration to include Epiphany, here are some ideas for doing so.

- Save one Christmas present for each family member to open on Epiphany. These gifts represent the gifts that the Magi gave to Jesus when they found Him. Choose one family member to dress up as one of the Wise Men to distribute the gifts. Let other family members help the Wise Man don his royal attire—Dad's bathrobe or a bath towel cape and a crown made from construction paper.

- Start the tradition of giving spiritual gifts on Epiphany. Make cards or slips of paper with one Christian virtue such as love, patience, faithfulness, or kindness written on each. Without being able to see what is on the cards, each family member draws a spiritual gift to nurture and work on during the coming year.

- As part of the day's festivities, make a special cake with a surprise baked inside such as a dried bean or nut. You can also use a small trinket that can withstand baking but does not present a choking hazard. The family member who finds the surprise in his piece of cake gets to be king for the rest of the day. In addition to any extra privileges you may choose, give the king the honor of offering a special prayer of blessing for the whole family.

- Invite friends over for an Epiphany party. As part of your celebration, play a game in which someone hides a small baby doll somewhere in the house. All of the guests are Wise Men except for one who plays the role of King Herod. The object of the game is for one of the Wise Men

50

to find the baby Jesus before Herod does. At the end of the party, ask everyone to go home by another route just as the Wise Men did to elude King Herod.

❏ During the evening of Epiphany, spend some time together outside gazing at the stars. Ask the children to point out stars they think look like the star the Wise Men followed. Talk about the excitement and joy the Wise Men must have felt when the star they were following finally stopped over Jesus' house.

❏ If your family uses an Advent candle with a Christ candle, light the Christ candle during the evening meal on each of the twelve days from Christmas until Epiphany. Let the light of the candle remind you that Jesus is the Light of the world and without Him, we would be in darkness.

~ *Part IV: Christmas Giving* ~

As extended families increase in size, the challenge of gift giving becomes even more complicated and expensive. The pressure to find the right gift for every aunt, uncle, niece, nephew and cousin can be overwhelming. The same scenario occurs in large offices or work groups. In these cases, the most practical solution for simplifying is to look for alternative methods of exchanging gifts.

Alternative Ideas to Traditional Gift Exchanges

One variation I have heard frequently is the one in which only the children in large extended families receive gifts. I never liked this idea because I think it encourages children to focus only on themselves. This method of gift exchange seems to only reinforce the "Gimme" and "I want" attitudes most parents wish to avoid. However, if everyone in your family agrees that this method works best, then by all means do what works for you.

Here are some other alternatives to traditional everyone-gives-everyone-else-a-present gift exchanges. Modify or combine any of these to suit your needs.

❑ Hold a yard sale or dollar store gift exchange. Another variation on this idea is to set a low dollar limit (such as $3-5) and see what kind of creative gifts participants can think up. To make things even simpler, draw names in advance so that each person has only one family member for whom to shop.

❑ Try a homemade gift exchange in which all gifts must be handmade. In addition to crafts, this could include food gifts or homemade coupons for services such as babysitting or housecleaning to be provided by the giver.

❑ Decide as a group that instead of giving gifts to each other, givers will give the amount that would have been spent on gifts to a charity in the recipient's honor. Be creative in choosing organizations that fit the recipient's interests and values.

- ❑ Set a small spending limit for gifts. Ask each person who wants to participate in the gift exchange to bring as many gifts as she would like to swap. Number the gifts and allow guests to draw as many numbers as the number of gifts they brought to exchange. This method is beneficial because it allows guests to opt out of the gift exchange if they so choose.
- ❑ Hold a gift exchange in which everyone brings a small gift to swap. Exchange gifts in some unorthodox fashion. One example would be to pass the gifts from person to person as music plays. When the music stops, each person keeps the gift she is holding.
- ❑ For larger groups such as work groups or Sunday school classes, have a gift exchange with an inexpensive theme such as a Christmas ornament or homemade candy exchange.
- ❑ For laughs, hold a gag gift exchange. In this gift swap, the more obnoxious and tacky, the better. Give a prize to whoever brings the most outrageous gift.
- ❑ Suggest a white elephant gift exchange in which participants bring off-the-wall items from around their homes to swap. Along the same lines as a white elephant exchange, host a recycled gift exchange. In this scenario, guests swap gifts they have received in the past that they could not use.
- ❑ Give gifts to each family represented rather than each individual. Choose items that can be enjoyed by all members of the family such as a board game or a gift basket of homemade snacks.

No matter what alternate route you choose, make sure everyone in the group agrees on it and understands the rules beforehand so that no one ends up hurt or disappointed. Also, it is good to decide early in the year—like at the family Memorial Day or Fourth of July picnic—how the Christmas gift exchange will be handled so everyone has plenty of time to prepare.

The Holiday Charity Dilemma: To Give or Not to Give

Before we leave this chapter on simplifying Christmas, I'd like to address the issue of holiday philanthropy. During the weeks between Thanksgiving and Christmas, opportunities for charitable giving abound. Everywhere you go, someone is asking you to donate something. Although giving to such organizations fulfills the O aspect in the formula for holiday joy (*pages 29-31*), the sheer volume of requests can be overwhelming.

As the holiday season approaches and I am faced with dozens of requests to contribute, I often find myself personally faced with a dilemma. Although I want to do my part, I can't help but question whether this kind of seasonal giving is truly the best use of my money. When I donate cash or Christmas toys to large organizations, how do I know that my gift is actually going to help those in need? How do I know that the organization goes about helping the needy in ways that are consistent with my values? And does this kind of charitable aid do anything to help recipients break out of, rather than perpetuate, the cycle of poverty and dependence on others?

> The most effective type of charity involves education. The poor must be taught to be independent, while givers must learn to give in ways that empower the poor to make positive changes in their lives.

Several years ago, I interviewed the administrators of a non-profit organization that offers career counseling and life skills training to the unemployed. The goal of this program is to help the chronically unemployed get back into the workforce and off of welfare. With years of experience in working with the poor, I knew these individuals could offer valuable insight into this issue of holiday charitable giving.

On the day of my visit, I started the interview by describing my mixed emotions about giving during the holiday season. They empathized and explained that these misgivings are understandable. In their daily work with the needy, they see many instances in which good intentions by individuals and agencies go awry. Many times the help given is shortsighted and can actually discourage recipients from trying to better themselves.

Unfortunately, many churches and government agencies tend to dole out money without any kind of restrictions or incentive for independence. In such a scenario, the needy will naturally stay dependent on others. In the long run, this kind of assistance is of little benefit in helping the poor help themselves. My interviewees stressed that the most effective type of charity involves education. The poor must be taught the necessary life skills to be independent, while givers must learn to give in ways that empower the poor to make positive changes in their lives.

Every year around the holiday season, this particular organization receives many calls from well-meaning families who want to adopt a low-income family during the holiday season. Although these people have good intentions, the administrators admitted they don't quite know what to do with these requests. This kind of one-time giving is more like a handout, which makes the givers feel good. A better approach is to give a hand-up—assistance that helps the recipients help themselves, which makes them feel good.

When asked to give guidelines to help givers choose which organizations to support during the Christmas holidays, my interviewees gave these suggestions.

Look for empowerment. What is the organization doing to help the poor help themselves? The best opportunities for giving assist the needy not only in taking care of their own families, but also in giving something back to society.

Are there checks and balances within the program? Does the organization truly know their clients and how to best help them? These checks and balances should include logistically being able to pull off what they wish to accomplish and enforcing limits so there is fairness and little chance of the system being abused.

Are there opportunities for involvement on the part of the giver? Certainly, some givers are content with making one-time donations and don't desire any further involvement. But for those who truly want to help bring about change in the lives of others, there should be opportunities to connect with those in need throughout the year, not just at Christmas.

Charitable giving can be a wonderful way to enrich your family's Christmas season. Using these guidelines will help you wade through the many donation requests you receive. But as you consider making donations of toys, food or cash, why not also consider the possibility of making a difference by giving some of your time and talent? Remember that personal involvement and active participation is always in season.

Chapter Three:
Saint Valentine's Day Simplified

*I*t seems rather ironic how far removed our modern Valentine's Day celebrations are from the original purpose and intent of this special day. Today, St. Valentine's Day is a time to remember our sweethearts and celebrate romantic love. While there is nothing wrong with this focus on romance, this kind of celebration is very different from how the holiday began. At its inception, February 14th was set aside to remember two Christian men, both named Valentine, who were martyred for their faith.

Church tradition holds that one of these two Valentines was a bishop executed for converting a Roman family to Christianity. The other Valentine was a priest jailed for aiding persecuted Christians. During his time in jail, he reportedly healed the jail keeper's daughter of her blindness. Legend holds that the night before his execution, St. Valentine wrote the young lady a note of affection and signed it, Your Valentine.

Honoring Christian martyrs is a far cry from wining and dining the object of your affection. Pope Gelasius founded St. Valentine's Day in 496AD to give Christian significance to a pagan festival. He would probably roll over in his grave if he knew that modern celebrations are more about fluff than faith.

Be My Simple Valentine

When you hear the words Valentine's Day, what images immediately come to mind? Bouquets of red or pink flowers? Foil boxes filled with delicious chocolates? Romantic cards containing sentimental words? Most likely, at least one of these images comes to you. But how about this one: money?

Even the concept of honoring the one you love has been soiled by this dirty, five-letter word that when spoken, hurls you from the fantasy world of passion and delight back to the everyday reality of budgeting and making ends meet. Alas, whether we like it or not, money is an integral part of how the Valentine's Day game is played. Every year, lovers everywhere spend millions of dollars on tangible symbols of their deepest affections.

Is this bad? Am I trying to take all the fun out of February 14th? Not at all. If it weren't for all the media hype and the blatant reminders everywhere you turn, some poor spouses might never receive tokens of their partners' love. Because of the hectic pace at which so many of us live, we often neglect one of the most basic tasks of strengthening and maintaining relationships. The immense media focus on Valentine's Day, commercialized as it may be, does serve the important function of reminding us all to express our affection and gratitude to the people who share our lives.

Expressing devotion to your loved one is good; blowing your budget on expensive flowers that soon wilt or a pricey dinner that lasts only a few hours is not so good. Note the key words here are blowing your budget. Please understand that I am not criticizing anyone who has the available resources and chooses to use them for these kinds of gifts.

The problem comes when money that should be used for savings or paying off debt is used for temporary pleasures. Most of us would agree that such gift giving does not do anything to simplify and enrich the quality of our lives. In fact, this kind of spending accomplishes just the opposite. Money worries only add to the pressure to work harder and earn more. Besides, if your budget is tight and both of you know it, your partner may find it difficult to enjoy an extravagant gift.

Another problem with this kind of celebration is when it is done not out of love, but because the participants feel pressure to celebrate by spending. If traditional Valentine's Day gifts don't mean anything to you, why should you feel obliged to give them or to act overjoyed when you receive them? Simplifying this celebration means finding ways to honor your loved one that reflect what is meaningful to you both.

We've seen that traditional ways of celebrating are not necessarily the best. But are there ways to show honor to your sweetie without doing damage to your budget? Is it possible to cut through the commercialism and express your love simply and sincerely?

Thankfully, the answer to both of these questions is a resounding "Yes!" In fact, you are probably smiling right now as you remember some special token given to you or that you have given during times when money was tight. You know from personal experience that with a little thought and creativity, you can express your love in ways that are far superior to a quick stop by the florist on the way home from work.

Let's face it. Anyone can shell out a great deal of money for a gift without much thought. But how many people can give thoughtful gifts without shelling out a great deal of money? Giving that kind of gift takes time, effort and a certain ingenuity many people are unwilling to take the time to nurture. When the effort is taken, however, the result is a heartwarming gift that is remembered for many years to come.

> Anyone can shell out a lot of money for a gift without much thought. But how many people can give thoughtful gifts without shelling out a lot of money?

A friend whose name is also Nancy once told me a story of a time when she and her husband had very little money around the time of their anniversary. She knew there wasn't even enough to buy an anniversary card so she decided to surprise her husband with a homemade card. As she tried to gather the construction paper, glue and markers to make the card, she was the one who was surprised. When she couldn't find the supplies and went looking, she found her husband busily using them to make a homemade card for her!

Even though the event happened many years ago, my friend still had a certain sparkle in her eyes and glow on her face that told me how special the memory was to her. Her husband had given her the gift of his time and his earnest desire to please her. His simple gift was not costly, but it was definitely priceless to Nancy.

Simplifying does not mean you scrimp on the generous outpouring of your love. Instead, you express that love in ways that reflect your values. Candy, flowers, dining out—there's nothing wrong with these things except the fact that retailers have a great deal to gain from convincing you that no Valentine's Day is complete without them. By putting your creativity to work, you can bypass the traditional route and give an eloquent expression of your love that won't drain your budget.

Million Dollar Gift Giving for Next to Nothing

What is a "million dollar gift"? It's not a 3-carat diamond ring or a shiny new Porsche in the driveway. It isn't a big screen TV or a new riding lawnmower. A million dollar gift is a simple yet meaningful gift that makes both the giver and the recipient feel like a million bucks!

Your loved one feels great because you took the time and effort to go beyond the ordinary to give an extraordinary token from your heart. You feel terrific because you were able to wow your sweetie without spending a large sum of money that could have been used for savings or paying off debt.

Let me give you a personal example of how it works. On the first Valentine's Day after we both left our jobs to become self-employed, my husband, Michael, and I agreed to try something different. To avoid spending a lot of money we wanted to save, we decided on a $5 limit per person on our Valentine's gifts. To a spendthrift, a $5 limit would have been like the kiss of death: *"What can I possibly buy for only five dollars?"* For us, it became a game: *"What kinds of cool stuff we can come up for with less than five dollars?"* Both of us enjoyed the challenge of searching out items that would fit the bill.

Michael is a woodworker, so for him it was easy. He used his time and only a little money to make me a beautiful oval frame for a wall mirror I already had. He used wood that was salvaged from discarded packing crates, 25¢ paint from a yard sale, and plans he drew up on his computer. The only thing he had to go out and buy was a dowel for putting the frame together, which cost only 76¢ at the hardware store. The end result was beautiful. My mirror with its new frame still hangs proudly in our bedroom.

For Michael, I found a Bible desk calendar that had a different scripture about love each day. Because it was February, the calendar was on clearance for $4. I also found a woodworking book at a library discard sale for 50¢. In addition, I made him a homemade card and a plate of his favorite cookies. When you add the cost of the cookie ingredients, I actually went over my limit just a little but he was delighted nonetheless. In fact, we both enjoyed our gifts and the thrill of the hunt so much that we instituted the five-dollar rule for other gift giving occasions such as birthdays and anniversaries as well.

Below I've listed a few of my own ideas for million dollar gifts. The suggestions are listed in two categories. *Time and Talent Gifts* are those that do not directly require any money, only your time and creativity and a few basic supplies you probably have lying around the house. *Thrifty Gifts* are those that require your time and less than $10. Use this list as a guide to help you come up with your own million dollar gifts for Valentine's Day or any other gift giving occasion.

Time and Talent Gifts

- ❏ Make an "I Love You Because..." jar. Decorate a recycled jar and fill it with individual slips of paper, each listing something you love and appreciate about your sweetheart. If you are really ambitious, you can come up with 365 things—one for each day until next Valentine's Day.

- ❏ Treat your loved one to a day or week off from duties such as housework, yard work, etc. What could be nicer for a stressed-out sweetie than a little time to relax?

- ❏ Volunteer to do a major task that your beloved either doesn't like or hasn't had time to do. Do that mountain of ironing. Clean out the garage. Paint the spare bedroom.

❑ Present your loved one with an IOU for an evening of your undivided attention. Explain that on that night, you'll be free to talk, listen, cook dinner, give a massage—whatever you sweetheart asks you to do.

❑ Arrange for your spouse to enjoy a long, luxurious bath. Make her feel like she's visiting a day spa by drawing the water and setting out the best towels. Light candles, dim the lights and make her a cup of her favorite warm beverage. Make yourself and the kids scarce, but be available just in case she needs anything.

Thrifty Gifts

❑ Using your computer's desktop publishing program and scanner, write a book about the history of your relationship. Include photos along with your recollections of how the relationship has grown and changed over time. When you finish, take your masterpiece to a copy shop to have it attractively bound.

❑ Shop at used bookstores, thrift shops or garage sales for gently used items that would make great gifts. A book by a favorite author. Old issues of a favorite magazine. A collectible to add to your spouse's collection.

❑ Have an enlargement made of a photo from a special time the two of you shared together. House the photograph in an inexpensive frame and present it with a handwritten note about a special memory you have from the day the photo was taken.

❑ Give your sweetie an ordinary food gift made in an extraordinary way. With the Valentine's Day theme in mind, whip up a heart-shaped homemade pizza, giant-sized cookie, or a decorated brownie with red and white frosting.

❑ Is there an old song that holds special significance in your relationship? What about a movie the two of you saw together in your early years of dating? Rekindle those fond memories by giving your loved one the album containing that song or the video of that particular movie.

Low-Cost Date Ideas (Not Just for Valentine's Day)

One of the keys to a strong, vibrant marriage is keeping that excitement, that certain sizzle the relationship had during the dating days. Think back to the earliest beginnings of your relationship with your mate. When you reminisce those precious times, most likely you'll recall the spontaneity and the sheer volume of hours spent just enjoying each other's presence.

At times when life is hectic and Michael and I become passing ships in the night, the best gift he could possibly give me is the gift of uninterrupted time to reconnect. During these much needed interludes, it doesn't matter too much what we are doing. What matters is that we are doing it together without the distractions of everyday life.

Consider the demands of life that have taken a toll on your relationship recently. Just as I crave time with my husband when life is chaotic, maybe your special someone also longs for some of your undivided attention. I can't tell you how much it always means to me when Michael sacrifices one of his most treasured commodities—his precious free time—to make time for just the two of us. Instead of giving something to each other, why not try doing something together as your Valentine's Day gift to each other? The low-cost ideas below are good for any occasion, but most would work particularly well during the cold winter month of February.

- ❑ Spend an afternoon dream building together. Is there some future purchase for which you are saving? Enjoy an afternoon of test driving cars, viewing model homes or window-shopping. This keeps you focused and motivated to press on toward your goal.
- ❑ Go to the library together. Check out books on a special topic or hobby that interests you both. Thumb through the books together over coffee at a nearby coffee shop or over a cup of tea in front of the fireplace at home.
- ❑ Put the kids to bed early and enjoy a candlelit dinner for two at home. Pull out the candles, the tablecloth and the best china. Cook a simple meal you both enjoy or try an exotic new recipe.

- Don't let a little precipitation spoil your fun. Don your raincoats, grab your umbrellas and go for walk in the rain. Better yet, use one umbrella for the two of you and snuggle close as you walk.
- Go on a duck feeding expedition at a park with a lake. Take along stale bread or crackers for the ducks and a thermos of hot coffee or cocoa for you.
- Work out as a couple. Go jogging, rollerblading or cycling in the park. The old sore muscles excuse is a great way to get or give a massage later that night.
- Pack a picnic lunch and go hiking at a state park. If it's too cold in your part of the country to have a picnic, find a place to park with a scenic view and eat in the car.
- Check the weekend edition of the newspaper for free entertainment such as an art exhibit, concert, or craft demonstration. Or sign up for a continuing education class on a topic that interests you both such as gourmet cooking or country line dancing.
- If your part of the country has snow in February, build a snowman or snow castle or make snow ice cream together. Or, if you're feeling particularly playful, have a snowball fight, but be sure to let your spouse win.
- How long has it been since either of you put on a pair of ice skates? Take your sweetie to the ice rink for an afternoon of fun. Be sure to hold hands while you skate like the other couples who are on dates.

Earning Valentine's Day Brownie Points for Paying Attention

If you've gotten nothing else out of this Valentine's Day discussion, I hope you are at least convinced that a romantic gift or a romantic time together does not have to be expensive. Throughout this book I have given a few examples of special gifts I have received over the years. All of the gifts I told you about had three things in common. First, they are all what I consider to be some of the most romantic gifts Michael has ever given me.

Next, each one cost Michael only a few dollars plus some of his time. Remember the beautiful frame Michael made for the cheap wall mirror I already had? The cost: only a couple of dollars worth of scrap wood, paint and a dowel. What about the sliding desk extension shelf I mentioned? Again, the only outlay for this gift was his time and a few dollars for basic supplies. And the magazine Michael tracked down because he knew I wanted a copy to keep for my scrapbook? The magazine was only a few dollars, but it probably took him a couple of hours to find a store with that particular issue in stock.

> As you make plans for Valentine's Day this year, try to surprise your sweetie with something uniquely personal that shows you have been paying attention.

The third commonality of these three gifts is that Michael showed his love by meeting an unspoken need or fulfilling a secret desire of mine. Without me having to beg or nag or write it down on my wish list, he noticed little indicators I gave as to what I would truly enjoy. As we discussed in Chapter One: *Meaningful Gift Giving*, this variety of thoughtfulness and attention to detail makes for a touching gift and an irresistibly romantic offering sure to win rave reviews.

Can you think of your own examples of how paying attention can help you give unforgettable tokens of your love? How about treating your spouse to a batch of cookies using the old recipe his grandmother used when he was a child? If your spouse has lost touch over the years with a special childhood friend, use the Internet to secretly track the person down and arrange for your spouse to receive an unexpected phone call or visit? Or why not make a scrapbook out of those precious old photos your loved one has never had time to put into albums?

As you make plans for Valentine's Day this year, try to surprise your sweetie with something uniquely personal that shows you have been paying attention. This kind of giving takes a little more effort than a last minute stop by the chocolate shop, but believe me, when you see the smile on your loved one's face, you'll know it was definitely worth it.

> Challenge yourselves to see how little you can spend without scrimping on any of the acts of kindness that express your true feelings for each other.

Avoiding Valentine's Day Letdown

Before we leave this chapter on Valentine's Day, there is one last issue I'd like to address. What if you and your partner have always gone overboard in the past? If you both have grown accustomed to making Valentine's Day a lavish affair, how do you simplify and scale back without diminishing the significance of the celebration?

There are no easy answers to these questions since every couple is unique and every relationship has its own special history. However, I do believe that to avoid disappointment and hurt feelings, it is critical to discuss the issue in advance and come to agreement on how the special occasion will be simplified.

If your sweetie is used to receiving a dozen long stem roses and a piece of jewelry for her collection each year, don't think that a plate of homemade cookies and a homemade card is going to cut the muster without some prior discussion. By the same token, if he looks forward to receiving a new power tool each February 14th, you can't just announce that you've decided to simplify and hand him an inexpensive gift without a little disappointment.

Having a common goal will help you come to agreement on this issue of scaling back. If you both agree that saving for a down payment on a house or getting out of debt by the end of the summer is most important, it should also be easy to agree on a small spending limit on Valentine's Day gifts.

Remember, too, that attitude is everything. If you view simplifying as depriving yourself, that's exactly how it will feel. Focus on what will be gained by adjusting your celebration, rather than what will be lost. Make it a game by challenging yourselves to see how little you can spend without scrimping on any of the little special touches and acts of kindness that express your true feelings for each other.

Chapter Four:
A Simpler Easter Celebration

*D*epending on how you were raised, Easter may or may not have had religious significance for you growing up. Personally, I was raised in a Christian family by parents who were very active in church. Yet, I don't remember much ever being said at church or at home about celebrating Easter as a spiritual holiday.

Easter for me was about coloring eggs, buying a new dress and eating a large meal that always included ham. It wasn't until I reached adulthood that I began to understand the true significance of the Easter observance. And even then, it wasn't until recent years that I learned about the special days leading up to Easter Sunday.

Looking back, I regret that for so many years I only experienced the commercialized, worldly exploitation of Easter. Unfortunately, the Easter Bunny was a more significant part of my celebration than Jesus Christ. Although there is nothing inherently wrong with hunting for eggs or dressing up in new clothes, I wish I had learned earlier what makes the Easter holiday different from other special occasions.

The Season of Lent

For some of you, the next couple of pages may be old hat. If you attend a church that follows the Church Calendar, you may already know the significance of the Lenten and Easter celebrations. If, like me, you were not taught these things as a child, the first step toward simplifying and adding meaning to your Easter celebration is to gain a basic understanding of all the special days within the Easter season.

The Lenten season is a period of 40 days beginning with Ash Wednesday and continuing through Easter. The period is actually a total of 46 days but Sundays are not considered part of Lent because they are already set aside as days of worship. Lent is a commemoration of the 40 days Jesus spent fasting and praying in the wilderness before he started his ministry.

The purpose of this observance is to reflect upon the suffering Jesus endured for us. It is also a time to re-examine our own commitment to follow and obey God regardless of the personal cost. It is a time of drawing close to Him through repentance and prayer. Just as Jesus fasted for forty days to prepare Himself for ministry, the Lenten season prepares us for ministering to the world as our response to what Jesus did for us.

Lent is traditionally a period during which Christians seek to separate themselves from the worldly influences that distract them from their relationship with God. To simulate Jesus' fasting, many people observe Lent by voluntarily abstaining from some food or activity that holds particular personal significance. In times past, Christians typically abstained from meat, eggs and dairy products during this period. Activities such as watching TV, drinking coffee and eating chocolate are modern examples of things people choose to give up during this period.

> The first step toward simplifying and adding meaning to your Easter celebration is to gain a basic understanding of all the special days within the Easter season.

Although not considered a holiday on the Church Calendar, the day before the Lent season begins is often referred to as Shrove Tuesday. Other names for this day are Fat Tuesday and Mardi Gras. Shrove Tuesday is a time of celebration and indulgence prior to the fasting of Lent. During the period when it was common to give up meat and dairy products during Lent, people would usually eat large quantities of these foods on Shrove Tuesday in order to use them up before Lent. Unfortunately, this indulgence has come to mean overindulgence to the extent that it is hard to believe that Mardi Gras is in any way connected to a spiritual holiday. A more suitable celebration would not include gluttony but rather the joyous partaking of whatever will be given up in order to make the fasting of Lent more meaningful.

Ash Wednesday is the first day of Lent and falls on the seventh Wednesday before Easter Sunday. This day derives its name from the ancient practice of putting ashes on one's head as a sign of mourning, repentance and humility before God. The focus of an Ash Wednesday church service is usually to remind listeners of their own sin and mortality. In some churches, a cross of ashes is placed on members' foreheads as a sign of mourning for Jesus' death and also for the spiritual death caused by man's sinfulness.

The Holy Days of Easter

Holy Week is the last week of Lent. Each of the special days in this week observes particular events in the last week of Jesus' life before His death. Palm Sunday marks the triumphant entry of Jesus into Jerusalem. According to the Gospel of John, the people greeted Jesus with shouts of joy and the waving of palm branches as He rode into town on a donkey. Hence, the atmosphere of Palm Sunday services is usually one of celebration. This Sunday is also referred to as Passion Sunday because it marks the beginning of Jesus' last difficult days leading up to His suffering on the cross.

The Holy Thursday or Maundy Thursday observance commemorates the events that took place the evening Jesus was arrested. During this night, Jesus instituted Communion by eating the Last Supper with His disciples. He also struggled in prayer in the Garden of Gethsemane and was betrayed by Judas Iscariot. Maundy Thursday services usually include Communion and focus on remembering the sadness and darkness Jesus experienced as He faced desertion by His closest friends and death on the cross. It is common for all altar adornments to be ceremoniously removed during the service. This stripping of the altar symbolizes the way Jesus was stripped of His clothing before crucifixion and also His abandonment by His followers.

71

Good Friday marks the arrest, trial, death and burial of Jesus. Church services on this day lead worshippers in experiencing some of the pain and humiliation Jesus experienced. Often churches have what is called Tenebrae, which is Latin for darkness or shadows. Typically throughout this Service of Shadows, lighting in the sanctuary is extinguished a little at a time until the room is completely dark, representing the death of Jesus and the hopelessness of man without God. A loud clanging of symbols represents the earthquake and the splitting of rocks that occurred at the moment of Jesus' death.

> How can we fully experience the exuberance of the Resurrection if we have not tasted any of the sorrow of the events leading up to it?

The last day of Holy Week is Holy Saturday. Corresponding to the Jewish Sabbath, this day commemorates the time Jesus rested in the tomb before his Resurrection on Easter Sunday. Historically this day is a day of meditation and contemplation. It is also used to remember the deceased and those who were martyred for their faith.

All of these special days lead up to the most exceptional day of all—the day we celebrate the Resurrection of our Lord and Savior. Without the Resurrection, the birth of Christ would lose its meaning. Easter is a joyous celebration of Jesus' victory over death and the new life we receive in Him because of His triumph. When celebrated against the backdrop of the darkness and mourning of Holy Week, Easter becomes a glorious proclamation of hope and God's love. That is why it is so important to understand the significance of the entire Easter season. How can we fully experience the exuberance of the Resurrection if we have not tasted the sorrow of the events leading up to it?

Adding Meaning to Your Easter Celebration

As a child, hunting eggs and eating chocolate bunnies were the main events in my Easter celebration. Now that I am a parent, I want my daughter to understand that the fun things people do at Easter time are merely festivities used to adorn what is already an extraordinary day. I want her to know that these festivities are icing on the proverbial cake, not the cake itself.

Making Jesus the center of the celebration can present a challenge when images of the Easter Bunny are so prevalent. Parents must take special measures to help kids understand that Jesus is the giver of Easter gifts—His love, His sacrificial death, the salvation we have through Him—not a big rabbit who hands out candy eggs. Here are some ideas for putting the spiritual significance back into your family's celebration.

❑ Put a spiritual twist on the tradition of decorating Easter eggs. Before dying the hard-boiled eggs, use crayons to write an Easter message on each egg. Because the wax of the crayons keeps the dye from adhering in those spots, your "Jesus is Risen" and "Jesus Died for You" messages will show through clearly.

❑ If your church does not celebrate Holy Week, attend Holy Week services at a church that does. Or celebrate each day as a family by reading passages of scripture that recount what each special day commemorates.

❑ Encourage each family member to observe Lent by giving up something of personal significance. Throughout the 40 days, talk about the meaning of sacrifice and what Jesus sacrificed for us.

❑ Attend an Easter cantata presented by a church other than the one your family normally attends. This allows family members to experience a celebration of Easter that is different than that to which they are accustomed.

❑ As a family, choose a few craft projects that emphasize the meaning of Easter. Do an Internet search or check out books from the library for ideas. Use your completed projects to decorate your home for your family celebration.

❑ Celebrate the Resurrection of Christ by doing the kinds of things Jesus came to earth to do. Extend God's love to others by visiting the elderly and sick, gathering up clothing to take to a homeless shelter, or making and delivering food baskets to families in need.

❑ Attend a sunrise service so your family can experience a little of what Jesus' followers must have felt the morning they found the empty tomb. Afterwards, enjoy a big family breakfast in celebration of the Risen Lord.

❑ Do some research on how the Resurrection is celebrated in other cultures. Turn the Easter celebration into even more of a learning experience by enjoying traditional Easter foods and activities from another country.

❑ Many churches make Easter crosses by attaching real flowers in some fashion to a wooden cross to symbolize the new life brought to us through Jesus' death. Make your own family Easter cross by cutting out a large cross from brown construction paper. Let the children use construction paper, markers, crayons and paint to create flowers to decorate it.

❑ Organize a Christian version of the Jewish Passover Seder. In the Jewish faith, the Passover Seder is a family celebration in which parents and grandparents teach the children about their faith by retelling the story of the Israelites' Exodus from Egypt. Your celebration can be very structured with traditional Passover foods and activities, or enjoy a simple meal as you spend time retelling the story of Jesus as our Passover Lamb. For additional information on hosting a Christian Passover, see Easter Resources in Chapter Eleven: *Resources.*

Tasty Treats that Teach a Lesson About Easter

Another way to add spiritual significance to the Easter celebration is to use the tradition of eating sweets to teach a spiritual lesson about the meaning of the holiday. Children are more likely to remember lessons that involve all of their senses in the learning process. The following recipes provide a fun opportunity to make the Resurrection story come to life through the senses of sight, taste, touch, hearing, and smell.

Resurrection Cookies

Ingredients You'll Need:
- ❑ 1 cup whole pecans
- ❑ 1 teaspoon vinegar
- ❑ 3 egg whites
- ❑ Pinch of salt
- ❑ 1 cup sugar

Supplies and Equipment You'll Need:
- ❑ Mixing bowl
- ❑ Zipper bag
- ❑ Wooden spoon
- ❑ Electric mixer
- ❑ Measuring cup and spoons
- ❑ Wax paper
- ❑ Cookie sheet
- ❑ Tape
- ❑ Bible

Instructions:
1. Preheat oven to 300 degrees Fahrenheit. It is important to do this at the very beginning, before you do anything else, so that the oven has plenty of time to heat.
2. Place pecans in plastic zipper bag. Let the children use the wooden spoon to beat the pecans and break them into small pieces. Read John 19:1-3. Talk with children about how Jesus was beaten by the soldiers after He was arrested.
3. Put 1 teaspoon of vinegar into mixing bowl. Let each child smell the vinegar. Read John 19:28-30. Explain to the children that when Jesus was thirsty as He hung on the cross, He was given vinegar to drink.
4. Add egg whites to vinegar. Read John 10:10-11. Tell the children that eggs represent life. Explain that Jesus gave His life to give us new life in Him and also eternal life.

5. Sprinkle a little salt into each child's hand. Let the children taste it and then brush the rest into the bowl. Read Luke 23:27. Tell them that this represents the salty tears shed by Jesus' followers when Jesus was crucified.

6. Add 1 cup of sugar. Explain that so far, the ingredients are not very appetizing. Read Psalm 34:8 and John 3:16. Tell the children the sweetest part of the story is that Jesus died for our sins because He loves us. He wants us to know and love Him, too.

7. Beat with a mixer on high speed for 12 to 15 minutes until the mixture forms stiff peaks. Read Isaiah 1:18 and John 3:1-3. Tell the children that the color white represents purity. Everyone who has been cleansed of his sins is pure in God's eyes.

8. Fold in broken nuts. Drop by rounded teaspoons onto a cookie sheet covered with wax paper. Read Matthew 27:57-60. Explain to the group that each mound represents the rocky tomb where Jesus' body was laid.

9. Put the cookie sheet in the oven, close the door and turn the oven off. Read Matthew 27:65-66. Talk about how Jesus' tomb was sealed. Give each child a piece of tape to seal the oven door.

10. Before going to bed, read John 16:20, 22. Tell the children that they may feel sad to leave the cookies in the oven overnight. Jesus' followers also felt very sad when the tomb was sealed.

11. The next morning, open the oven and let each child take a cookie. Notice the cracked surface. Take a bite and you will find that the cookies are hollow! Read Matthew 28:1-9. Tell the children that on the first Resurrection day, Jesus' followers were amazed to find the tomb open and empty. Lead the children in a prayer of thanksgiving to God that Jesus is risen.

Resurrection Rolls

Ingredients You'll Need:
- ❑ 1 can refrigerated crescent roll dough
- ❑ Melted butter or margarine
- ❑ Large marshmallows
- ❑ Cinnamon
- ❑ Sugar

Supplies and Equipment You'll Need:
- ❑ Bowls for the butter and the cinnamon and sugar mixture
- ❑ Non-stick cooking spray or oil
- ❑ Cookie sheet
- ❑ Bible

Instructions:
1. Preheat the oven to 350 degrees Fahrenheit. Read John 19:38-42. Open the can of crescent rolls and separate into triangles. The rolls represent the linen that Joseph of Arimethea and Nicodemus used to wrap Jesus' body.
2. Dip each marshmallow in the melted butter. Then roll the marshmallows in the mixture of cinnamon and sugar. This represents the oils and spices Joseph and Nicodemus used to anoint Jesus' body for burial.
3. Place each marshmallow in the center of a crescent triangle. Fold the dough around the marshmallow to completely cover it. Pinch the edges tightly to seal the marshmallows within the dough. Put each crescent on a lightly greased cookie sheet. This represents how Jesus' body was wrapped carefully and laid in the tomb.
4. Bake the rolls for 10 to 12 minutes. This represents the time Jesus' body was in the tomb.
5. Read Matthew 28:1-7. When the rolls have baked and cooled slightly, let each child take a roll and open it. In the same way that Mary Magdalene and the other Mary discovered Jesus was not in the tomb, the children will also find that the marshmallow in each roll is gone. During baking, the marshmallows melt and the crescent rolls puff up. Just like Jesus' tomb, the rolls are empty!

Ideas for Simplifying the Easter Celebration

When you think about the significance of the Lenten and Easter seasons, you realize what a pity it is that this glorious time has been exploited commercially. Sellers of greeting cards, flowers, candy, and gifts have tried to turn Easter into another Christmas. How sad that such a sacred holiday should become just another avenue for consumerism!

If you want to simplify and enrich your Easter celebration, consider these ideas that focus on replacing the commercial aspects of the holiday with activities that are more in keeping with the spirit of the season.

- ❏ Rather than the traditional Easter decorations with images of bunnies, chicks and eggs, make your own decorations using symbols of your faith. Images of Jesus, the cross and the empty tomb all depict the true meaning of the Easter celebration.

- ❏ Make your own greeting cards with messages that proclaim the wonderful news of Jesus' Resurrection. Use your computer's desktop publishing program or crayons, markers and construction paper to make Easter cards for friends and relatives.

- ❏ If you do buy gifts for the children in your family, stick with a spiritual rather than secular theme. Consider giving coloring books, bookmarks, stickers and toys that convey the Easter message. Check Christian bookstores for these kinds of gifts.

- ❏ If you choose to use flowers as part of your celebration, keep arrangements simple. A modest corsage or arrangement of flowers from your own garden makes a much clearer statement of your values than an expensive purchase from the floral shop.

- ❏ Instead of spending a great deal of money on chocolate and other prepackaged candy, make homemade cookies and other sweets to be enjoyed as part of the holiday. See the previous section, *Tasty Treats that Teach a Lesson about Easter,* for ideas.

❑ If receiving new clothes is part of your family tradition, consider sewing them by hand. If making an outfit is too big of an undertaking, consider making one special accessory like a hair bow, tie, sash or piece of simple jewelry to adorn an outfit you already have.

❑ Rather than serving an elaborate meal with all the trimmings, consider serving a modest meal and donating the extra money you would have spent to an organization that feeds the hungry.

Chapter Five:
A Simpler Approach to Mother's Day
and Father's Day

*M*other's Day as we know it dates back to 1907 when Anna Jarvis from West Virginia held a service to honor her mother. The idea quickly caught on and in the year 1914, President Woodrow Wilson declared the second Sunday in May to be Mother's Day.

Not wanting fathers to be left out, Sonora Dodd of Spokane, Washington held the first service honoring her dad in June of 1910. She chose June because it was the month of her dad's birthday. Although President Calvin Coolidge supported the idea of Father's Day, it didn't become official for another 56 years. In 1966, President Lyndon Johnson proclaimed the third Sunday in June as Father's Day. In 1972, President Richard Nixon made the holiday a permanent national observance.

What started out as simple memorial services to honor mothers and fathers has now become a multimillion-dollar moneymaker for the flower, gift and greeting card industries. If you have ever found yourself irritated at how commercialized holidays have become, just think how Mother's Day founder Anna Jarvis must have felt. The story goes that she was so bitter over exploitation of her original idea that she actually filed a lawsuit to have one Mother's Day event stopped. She was also arrested for disturbing the peace at another event where carnations were being sold. Now that's what I call irritation!

As with most holidays that get out of hand, the intent of these special occasions is honorable, but the extent to which they have been exploited is regrettable. Ads for Mother's and Father's Day promotions slyly suggest that you're not paying proper respect to your parents if you don't spend a large chunk of change doing it. Thankfully, this propaganda is not true. What most parents really want is not more stuff, but more of you—your time, your love and your true emotions expressed in meaningful ways.

81

Creatively Simple Mother's Day Gift Ideas

We all agree that our moms are marvelous. We don't need prompts from the greeting card industry to remind us of that. The dilemma is how to make them feel marvelous without buying into all the hype surrounding Mom's special day.

A few years ago before I became a mother myself, I wanted to get the inside scoop on what moms really want for Mother's Day. What brings them happiness? What makes them feel appreciated? To do this, I enlisted the help of a group of women I met online. I asked them for inexpensive gift ideas that either they have received or would love to receive themselves, or that they have given their own mothers in the past.

Their suggestions fell into two categories: things to give to Mom and things to do for Mom. Below you will find a synopsis of the ideas I received. As you look over the list, remember that most of these ideas are adaptable and can be used for the fabulous fathers or the grand grandparents on your list as well.

Things to Give to Mom

- ❑ Homemade Bath Products – Honor Mom by treating her to a little luxury and relaxation. Search the library or Internet for recipes to make your own bath oils, bath salts, bubble bath or soaps. If finding time to actually use these products is a problem, include a homemade coupon for some babysitting or housecleaning so she can take time to enjoy herself.
- ❑ Children's Artwork – What mom doesn't love the gifts her children make for her? Children's drawings, paintings or poems all become extra special when placed in an attractive frame.
- ❑ A Hobby Basket – What does your mom do for fun? Create a gift basket using her hobby as a theme. For example, if she loves to play sports, create a gift basket with a new water bottle, a book on fitness, and several new pairs of athletic socks.
- ❑ Roses – Most women love roses, right? Rather than giving her a bouquet that she can only enjoy for a few days, give her a rose bush that will bloom for years to

come. If you want, include an IOU good for a few hours of gardening time to help her plant your gift in her flower garden.

- ❑ Handprints or Footprints – Use her children's hands or feet to make a memorable gift. The impression of a child's hand or foot can be pressed into modeling clay to make a wall hanging or quick drying cement to make a garden stepping stone. You can also coat the palm of the child's hand or the sole of his foot with washable ink or paint. Then stamp the print onto cardstock to create a keepsake suitable for framing.

- ❑ A "Thanks, Mom" Book – On each page of a blank journal, write a message of thanks such as, "Thank you for always encouraging me," or something about your mom for which you are thankful like, "I am thankful that you taught me the value of hard work." Include a note that instructs Mom to reread this book often to remind her of how much she is loved and appreciated.

- ❑ A Personalized Apron – Use fabric paint or iron-on transfers for your inkjet printer to create an apron that is just Mom's style. Decorate the apron with family photos or stenciled decorations.

- ❑ Chocolate Fantasy – Is Mom a chocolate fanatic? Fill a gift basket with several varieties of homemade cookies, candy and muffins in her favorite flavor. If Mom loves sweets but is concerned about her weight, use recipes for special goodies that are low in fat and sugar.

Things to Do for Mom

- ❑ Spring Cleaning – Devote a few days of your time doing cleaning tasks over and above the ones she does on a regular basis. This could include steam cleaning the carpets, taking down and washing curtains, washing windows, defrosting the freezer, etc.

- ❑ Give Her a Mini-Vacation – Arrange for Mom to enjoy an overnight getaway to visit friends or relatives in another city. Or take the kids on a weekend camping trip so that she can have plenty of time at home for all those fun projects she never has time to do.

❏ Handyman Services – If your mom lives alone, basic home maintenance may be overwhelming to her. Volunteer a day or weekend of your time to complete those things she cannot do herself or cannot afford to pay someone else to do such as painting, pruning, or doing repairs around her home.

❏ Do the Cooking for Her – Prepare a freezer full of homemade meals that she can heat and serve. If she lives alone, this can be easily accomplished by simply freezing an individual-sized portion from each of the meals you cook for your own family for a few weeks. Or if she has more people than just herself to cook for, double your dinner recipes and freeze the extra portions in oven-safe or microwave-safe containers.

❏ Complete a Special Project – Is there a project she has wanted done for a long time that she can never find time to do? Ideas that would fit in this category include refinishing a piece of furniture, wallpapering a room in her house, remodeling a bathroom, etc.

Any of these low-cost, high-value gift ideas are sure to bring a smile to the face of the special mom in your life. Or, if you are a mother who thinks your family may need a little help with Mother's Day gift giving, you have my permission to make several copies of this list and leave them in conspicuous places around the house!

Frugal Father's Day Gift Ideas

For many women, the fathers on their gift lists present the biggest gift giving challenges. Men don't seem to have this problem. Being of the male species themselves, they usually have special insight into what their dads would enjoy.

If you are one of those who has trouble knowing what to get dear old Dad, look over the following list of gift ideas that also fall into the simple, yet meaningful category.

- ❑ The Gift of Laughter – Is there some old comedian or sitcom that always makes him chuckle? Use your VCR to make a tape of as many episodes as you can record. When you give your gift, include a note instructing him to watch it anytime he needs a good laugh.

- ❑ Dad's Own Webpage – Use your scanner and computer skills to create a homepage devoted to all Dad's many interests. Include pictures of his children, hobbies and accomplishments. Tell how proud you are of him and how grateful you feel to have him as your father. After you've uploaded the site with the help of your Internet Service Provider, include the URL in a card telling Dad to visit that webpage for a special surprise.

- ❑ The Gift of a Clean House – If your dad lives alone, housecleaning may not be high on his list of priorities. If possible, surprise him by giving his home a good, thorough cleaning while he is away for a few days. Even if you can't surprise him, he is sure to enjoy the results when you finish.

- ❑ The Gift of Encouragement – Find a special quote or Bible verse that is particularly meaningful. If you are handy with a needle and embroidery floss, create a cross-stitch sampler featuring those words. If not, use your calligraphy skills and put the verse in an attractive frame to sit proudly on his desk at work.

- ❑ A Subscription to His Hometown Newspaper – This gift may cost a little more but is sure to be a winner. If he no longer lives in the small town where he grew up, purchase a gift subscription to that town's local newspaper. This gift will help him keep up with the happenings in the place he used to call home.

Several of these ideas are ones that worked well with my own hard-to-gift father. Of course, they can be modified for any other family member—male or female—who presents a gift buying challenge.

Gifts that Keep Giving

One of the dilemmas of choosing gifts for parents or grandparents is that in many cases, these family members are well established and financially secure. If there is anything they really need or want, they can probably easily afford to buy it themselves. And unlike young people who have unique needs associated with each new phase of their lives, parents have many years of living under their belts and usually already own more stuff than they can ever actually use or enjoy.

What do you get someone who has everything? This chapter on Mother's Day and Father's Day gift giving seems like an appropriate place to share another gift idea that goes above and beyond the ordinary. I like to call this category of presents "gifts that keep giving."

I discovered this variety of gift giving one year when I was particularly stumped on what to get my dad for his birthday. After pondering what Dad would truly enjoy and put to good use, I remembered that he loves all kinds of baked goods. He is particularly fond of a certain style of yeast rolls I usually make for family gatherings. Instead of giving him some expensive gadget or gizmo, I decided to give him something he would really love: six months of his choice of homemade treats.

On his birthday, I made a batch of his beloved rolls. I used a basket I found at a yard sale and lined it with a cloth napkin and plastic wrap. I placed the rolls in the basket and covered them with more plastic wrap and another napkin. Using some ribbon that I also bought at a yard sale, I made a bow and attached it to the basket handle.

I presented the basket of rolls along with a gift certificate I made using my computer. The certificate explained that once a month for the next six months, my dad would receive his choice of fresh, homemade baked goods delivered right to his doorstep. At the beginning of the month, I would call to get his selection and then deliver it in a few days.

This plan worked like a dream. Each month when I brought whatever treat he chose, Dad felt like we were celebrating his birthday all over again. He felt honored I would take time out of my busy schedule to do something just for him. Each time he said, "This is the best gift you could have possibly given me."

This gift was also a winner for me for several reasons. During those six months, I spent more time with him than I normally would have. This gift was inexpensive, too. All it cost was the price of the ingredients and the gas to drive the treats over to him. I even learned some new recipes in the process.

When faced with the challenge of finding a gift for the person with everything, ask yourself if there is some way you can give a gift that keeps giving like the one I described. Maybe your father would love having one special home-cooked meal a week delivered to his door for the next month. How about one day out per month for the parent who is caring for his own elderly parents? What about a day per month of running errands if your parent doesn't drive? Use your creativity to come up with your own perfect gift for that extraordinary person for whom an ordinary gift just won't do.

> When faced with the challenge of finding a gift for the person who has everything, ask yourself if there is some way you can give a gift that keeps giving.

Gifts that Don't Create Clutter

Certainly the clutter factor should be a consideration on any gift giving occasion, but I believe it is especially important to mention it in connection with Mother's Day and Father's Day. Because parents do typically have more than enough of everything they need, special consideration should be given to ensure that your gift does not add to household clutter.

Gifts given by children or grandchildren hold a certain sentimental value that may make it difficult for the parents to ever let them go, even if their homes are already filled to capacity with other such gifts. This creates a gift giving dilemma for children. When faced with this challenge, homemade gifts seem to be a good alternative. However, many handmade gifts fit into the category of knickknacks, which is something most older people definitely don't need more of.

Another very practical solution to this challenge is to give gifts that are consumable. Gifts that can be eaten or used up are appreciated because they don't add to the problem of clutter. Consider also giving things that aren't really things at all, but rather experiences for the recipient to enjoy. In doing so, you give the gift of pleasant memories.

> To avoid giving Mother's Day and Father's Day gifts that create clutter, focus on functional items that the recipient can put to immediate use.

In your efforts to give non-cluttering gifts, you can still give homemade gifts that are creative and inexpensive. Many of the gift ideas listed throughout this book are edible. Food gifts definitely fall into the consumable category, as well homemade candles, potpourri or bath and body products. To avoid giving craft gifts that clutter, focus on making functional items that the recipient can put to immediate use. As for giving the gift of experience, almost all of the ideas that involve doing something for the recipient fill the bill nicely.

Even gifts that are store-bought can be both consumable and cost efficient. Look over the list below of non-cluttering gift ideas. You will find that most of them are universally welcome because they are items almost everyone uses. While some of these gift ideas are less expensive than others, you will surely find ideas to fit everybody and every budget.

Perishable, Use-It-Up Gifts

Personal Care Products

- ❏ Perfume
- ❏ Hand and body lotions
- ❏ Makeup
- ❏ Bath products (soaps, bath oils, shower gel, bubble bath)
- ❏ Nail care items (nail polish, cuticle cream, polish remover)

Food Gifts

- ❏ Fruit and nuts
- ❏ Flavored bread or bread mixes
- ❏ Wine, champagne, liqueur
- ❏ Flavored oils and vinegar
- ❏ Gourmet coffees and teas
- ❏ Gourmet sauces and flavorings
- ❏ Flavored coffees and creamers
- ❏ Hot cocoa mixes
- ❏ Unusual varieties of pasta
- ❏ Gourmet spices
- ❏ Ice cream toppings
- ❏ Chocolate

Household Items

- ❏ Stationery and stamps
- ❏ Candles
- ❏ Long distance phone cards
- ❏ Film or disposable cameras
- ❏ Recipe cards
- ❏ A computer program the recipient would use
- ❏ Dishcloths, bath towels, sheets and pillowcases

Miscellaneous Consumable Gifts

- ❏ Flowers
- ❏ Plants or flower bulbs
- ❏ Birdseed
- ❏ Magazine or newspaper subscriptions
- ❏ Calendars

Gifts of Experience

Gift Certificates
- ☐ Restaurant
- ☐ Grocery store
- ☐ Department, clothing or specialty store
- ☐ Hardware store or home improvement center
- ☐ Movie theater or video rental
- ☐ Yogurt or ice cream shop
- ☐ Entertainment coupon books
- ☐ Gift certificates for a manicure, pedicure, or massage
- ☐ Classes on topics related to recipient's interests/hobbies

Memberships/Season Passes
- ☐ Zoo or aquarium
- ☐ Opera, symphony or community theater
- ☐ YMCA or health club
- ☐ Amusement park
- ☐ Art museum
- ☐ Botanical gardens

Tickets
- ☐ Sporting events
- ☐ Concerts
- ☐ Exhibitions
- ☐ Theater productions
- ☐ Festivals
- ☐ Seminars
- ☐ Helicopter or hot air balloon rides

One final note about clutter-free giving. In giving consumable gifts, take extra care in selecting the manner in which you present your gift. In theory, presenting your gift in a reusable container is a good idea, but ask yourself if the recipient will actually reuse it. Be mindful that she may have trouble disposing of that decorative jar or pretty basket and may simply add it to the score of others she has around the house. If this is the case, avoid cluttering our landfills by choosing disposable packaging that can be thrown in a recycle bin after the gift is consumed.

Chapter Six:
Simplifying the Wedding Celebration

"White lace and promises,
A kiss for luck and we're on our way.
We've only just begun..."
"We've Only Just Begun"
Paul Williams and Roger Nichols

*S*weet and simple. That's how the marriage celebration is supposed to be. Ideally, every couple's wedding day should be a blissful commemoration marking the start of a long and prosperous life together. The wedding day, as well as the days leading up to it, should be filled with pleasant memories and time for reflecting upon the magnitude of the commitment the lovers will make. The wedding affair should accurately reflect not only the bride and groom's love for each other, but also the sanctity of the vows they make in the presence of God and loved ones.

Most women dream of their wedding day from the time they are old enough as little girls to say the words, "I do." They dream of being a princess for a day, whisked away by their own Prince Charming. They dream of feeling beautiful and honored and cherished. They want their special day to be unforgettable and magical. In short, they want everything to be perfect.

Brides dream of perfection, and the wedding industry responds by peddling the myth of perfection ruthlessly. Retailers and service providers know that even at times when the economy is slow, starry-eyed couples and their parents will shell out grand sums of money in an attempt to purchase a slice of this fantasy. But just as a perfectly flawless man or woman does not exist, perfect weddings exist only in fairy tales, soap operas and the world of marketing.

Cultural Issues With Wedding Celebrations

In the chapter on simplifying Christmas, we talked about the variety of conflicts couched within the Yuletide celebration. Wedding festivities as they are typically celebrated in America also have their share of inherent issues just waiting to burst the happy couple's bubble of bliss.

First, there is the difficulty of wedding planning. As if the stress of ending one phase of life and beginning another is not enough, the act of planning the wedding often tests the couple's endurance and ability to hold up under stress. There are so many details to attend to, so many decisions to make. How can the happy couple possibly relax and enjoy the last of their dating days when they feel so much pressure to orchestrate a major wedding production?

> All of the stress that usually accompanies the planning process can easily turn the wedding of the couple's dreams into an ordeal that is anything but dreamy.

And all of this orchestration doesn't come cheap, either. Even if the couple truly wants to keep costs down, wedding bills can quickly spiral out of control. The bride and groom may feel they must choose between the wedding they want and having the wedding they can afford. How can the couple experience all the joy of this major life event when anxiety over wedding expenses threatens to quickly snuff it out?

Family conflicts can also present a unique challenge. A wedding is supposed to be a time of rejoicing and bringing the family together, but existing tensions between family members don't magically disappear during this extraordinary time. In fact, these tensions are more likely to escalate during the busy weeks before the wedding. The bride and groom may find it difficult to relish their special day if they worry about estranged family members acting uncivilly toward one another during the wedding festivities.

In addition to these concerns, societal and family pressures to celebrate with rituals the couple would rather avoid can seem insurmountable. The bride and groom may feel their wedding is not really *their* wedding after all. Parents often believe it is their right to have a say-so in decision making if they pay part of the expenses. Even if they don't contribute financially, parents may contribute more than their share of unsolicited advice on how things should be done. The bride and groom are then faced with the delicate balancing act of trying to keep everyone happy. All of this stress can easily turn the wedding of their dreams into an ordeal that is anything but dreamy.

My Dream Wedding

Although we have now been married for eight years, it seems like only a few years have passed since Michael and I were planning our wedding. I had just completed a yearlong teaching assignment in Japan. Although I saved a tidy sum of money while working overseas, we were by no means on an unlimited budget. It was much more important to us to start our married life with money in the bank than to have an extravagant wedding that would leave us flat broke.

The challenge we faced in planning our wedding was getting what we both wanted while keeping the cost to a minimum. This sounds simple enough, but the problem was that what was important to me was not necessarily important to Michael, and vice versa. This disparity between what we each deemed necessary resulted in more than one tense discussion in the weeks before our wedding.

For example, Michael did not want to rent a tuxedo or buy a new suit for the wedding. "I've already got a whole closet full of suits I never wear," he said. "Why spend money on another?" Although we agreed to print the invitations ourselves using his computer, he couldn't understand why I wanted to purchase the cardstock and envelopes from a printer. He also felt that buying decorative napkins was silly when, in his opinion, cheap paper napkins would work just fine.

Thankfully, there were plenty of things on which we did agree. As I said, we both agreed that we would not go into debt to pay for our wedding. We also agreed that our wedding ceremony would be a small, intimate affair at his parents' home with only our families present. We decided to spend the majority of our money on a reception afterward for all of our friends to attend. Instead of the honeymoon cruise we originally planned, we opted to save our money and spend the week visiting several sights of interest in the region.

When all was said and done, we had our dream wedding. The ceremony was touching, the reception was beautiful and our honeymoon was fantastic. Despite the stress of the planning process, our wedding truly was unforgettable. For me, one of the best parts was when Michael, the one who would have been perfectly content to go to the Justice of the Peace, later said, "You know, Nancy, our wedding was wonderful. I wouldn't have changed a thing."

Knowing that Michael was pleased with everything about our wedding despite our initial disagreements was the best wedding gift I could have possibly received. However, the fact that our wedding was pleasing to both of us was not coincidental. We worked long and hard to find workable wedding solutions that fit both our personalities and our budget. In the end, our hard work paid off in the form of a celebration that made a statement about who we are and what is important to us.

Having the Wedding of Your Dreams

What would you do if someone gave you $20,000? Think about it for a minute. Maybe you would buy a new car or pay off an old debt. Perhaps you would use it as a down payment on a house or for the trip you always wanted to take but could never afford. Considering all the ways you could spend such a windfall, how would using it for an elaborate wedding rank on your list of possibilities?

According to information recently published in *USA Today*, $20,000 is what the average wedding in America now costs—the price of a new car or a down payment on a home. Wedding products and services now comprise an estimated $45 billion dollar a year industry. It seems our country has gone wedding crazy! Either that, or canny marketers have duped the public into thinking that no wedding is complete without hundreds of dollars worth of flowers or a $50 per person catered reception.

Thankfully, not everyone buys into this myth that spending a fortune is necessary to have a memorable wedding. Many couples, even those who could easily afford to go all out, opt for simpler weddings that more accurately reflect what they want their special day to be. Consequently, many valuable resources are available for those couples who would rather use their money for something other than a $20,000 wedding. For a list of helpful books and websites, see Wedding Resources in Chapter Eleven: *Resources*.

> A meaningful wedding is a direct result of the time and energy you invest in determining what you truly want out of the occasion.

It's All About You

Your wedding day is something for which you and your fiancé have waited a long time. Even if your engagement was short, many years of growth and learning have brought you both to the point of committing your lives to another person. It's your big day. Therefore, the event should be a reflection of both of you: your tastes, your preferences and your personalities. Your wedding should symbolize not only the love you have for each other, but also what you esteem most in your relationship. All too often, couples do not take time to thoroughly consider the statement they want their wedding to make. As a result, the event becomes a cookie cutter version of the latest wedding trend.

Because your wedding is such a personal statement of who you are, the most important part of the planning process has nothing to do with which church to reserve or who does your flowers. The pre-planning phase in which you devote time and energy to determining what you truly want out of the occasion is much more critical than the handling of aesthetic details. What do you want your wedding ceremony to say to guests? How do you want to remember this celebration? With all of the excitement and flurry of activity, it is tempting to skim over this step and allow tradition or someone else's opinion to dictate the details of your special day.

When planning a wedding on a budget, contrasting what you truly want your wedding to be against what everyone else is doing is essential. When funds are limited, you don't want to waste a big chunk of your wedding budget on elaborate food or expensive invitations if those things hold little value to you. Carefully choosing how you spend your money makes the difference between an unforgettable wedding and one where you later wonder, "Why did we spend so much?" Even if money is not so much of a concern for you, the careful thought you do beforehand helps you avoid mindlessly spending for extras that don't add significant value to your wedding experience.

What's Your Pleasure?

As you begin this pre-planning evaluation process, both you and your fiancé should ask yourselves these simple questions.

- ❏ What elements are important in making our wedding day memorable to me?
- ❏ Which of these are essential?
- ❏ Which of these are negotiable?

The purpose of these questions is to help you define exactly what it will take for both of you to walk away with a memorable wedding experience. For example, the bride may have always dreamed of wearing a long flowing gown and walking down the aisle of a church, but not feel quite as strongly about inviting a large group of friends and relatives to witness the event. By the same token, the groom may feel that above all other things, his wedding experience wouldn't be complete without having his best buddies from college as his groomsmen. He may also feel that having a live band at the reception is desirable, but not nearly as critical as being surrounded by friends on his big day.

Taking the time to answer these questions both individually and as a couple is important because it gives you a basic guide for allotting your money. As you think about your answers, consider the role family members' desires play in your wedding. Although your wedding is your special day, be realistic as you estimate how much other people's opinions influence decision making.

The next step is for both you and your fiancé to prioritize the items on your lists. Within the groups of essential and negotiable items, rank each item in order of importance. A simple way to do this is to give the highest ranking to the item on your list that you want more than anything else. Then continue asking yourself, "Which of these items do I want more than any of the remaining items on the list?" until each item on your list has been ranked.

> With patience, persistence and creativity, you can devise a plan that will fulfill what both of you desire from the wedding experience.

When comparing lists of what you both feel is essential, the process of planning out the details is simpler if your lists are similar. However, if your idea of what is most important is vastly different from your fiancé's, don't be discouraged. You can work together and come to agreement. You will just need to engage in some creative brainstorming. The goal is to arrive at a win-win scenario in which you both get what is most important to you.

If it is crucial to you to have a church wedding but your fiancé wants to keep it small, compromise by holding the service in a small church with only family and a few friends present. If he really wants to invite everyone he knows but you are concerned about the added expense, consider limiting the reception food to cake and punch. With patience, persistence and creativity, you can devise a plan that will fulfill what both of you desire from the wedding experience.

Making Your Dream Wedding a Reality

After you and your fiancé have negotiated and brainstormed for win-win scenarios which allow both of you to have what you want, you can then proceed with planning the details of your dream wedding. How you go about planning is largely influenced by your financial limitations. If you can afford more than you actually care to spend, your task is relatively easy. Your goal is to keep costs down by keeping things simple. Therefore, try to get the best value you can on the essentials and look for ways to scale back the negotiable items on your lists. As you plan, let your guiding thoughts be "Is this what we really want?" and "Is there a less expensive way to get the same effect?"

If you are on a limited budget, you should look for the least expensive ways to include all of the things you and your fiancé deemed essential so that there is money left in your budget for as many of the negotiable items as possible. That is where the ranking you did previously serves its purpose. Starting with your list of essentials, allot your money in order of importance so you are sure to get the critical details covered first. Let your guiding thought be "How can we creatively stretch our money so we can have most, if not all, of the things we truly want?"

Above all, don't lose sight of the ultimate meaning of your special day—two people in love committing their lives to each other. Ten years from now, no one will care what kind of gown you wore or if your flowers were fresh or silk. You will be just as married and just as happy regardless. So go ahead, plan your dream wedding and have fun doing it. Just don't allow the true meaning of this awesome celebration to get lost in the shuffle.

Practical Ways to Save on Wedding Expenses

Depending on your wedding budget, your efforts to simplify may range from scaling back slightly to bare bones simplification. Or you may choose to cut expenses to the minimum in one area so you can splurge on something else that holds more meaning. Whatever your goals, use the following savings ideas to get you started.

General Guidelines to Remember

- ❑ Borrow, borrow, borrow. Tablecloths, punchbowls, folding chairs, candleholders and even clothing items such as the bride's dress and veil can be borrowed to save you money. Friends are usually more than willing to help out when you ask well in advance.

- ❑ Avoid the wedding busy season if at all possible. Exact months vary by region of the country but the busiest wedding months are usually between May and October. Keep in mind that couples who marry in traditional wedding months are likely to spend more and have a more difficult time finding the services they desire. Weddings around the Christmas holidays are often pricey as well because of the competition for banquet facilities from large groups holding parties. By choosing to marry in one of the off-season months, you can usually negotiate better prices.

- ❑ Just as you should avoid busy months to save big, choosing a day other than Saturday for your wedding can also yield impressive savings. If you want to have your wedding on a weekend, consider a Friday night or Sunday afternoon wedding. Even on Saturday, a mid-morning or mid-afternoon time slot will be less popular and therefore less expensive than an evening affair.

- ❑ Do it yourself and save. It almost goes without saying that the more services you handle yourself, the more you will save. In addition to your own talents, think about friends and relatives who have special skills. Again, the key is to ask. Let friends know that their help with floral arrangements or food preparation or music would make a wonderful gift you would truly appreciate.

- ❑ Keep it simple. If you are on a tight budget, continuously ask yourself, "How can I do the same thing in a simpler fashion?" Less attendants, fewer guests, simpler flower arrangements. Remember that less truly is more. When it is all over, you will be glad you showed restraint.

❑ Consider using service providers who work out of their homes. Just because the person doesn't have a fancy photography studio or a floral shop of her own doesn't mean that the service you receive will be anything less than professional. Because these businesspeople keep their operations simple with low overheads, they should be able to pass those savings along to you.

❑ Look for service providers who offer deals including free services for which you would normally have to pay. A florist may offer to throw in the boutonnieres for free if you purchase all your other arrangements from him. The tuxedo shop may give a certain number of free wedding invitations with your tuxedo rental order.

❑ Remember that anything with the word wedding in it usually costs more. For example, a restaurant may quote a higher price for catering a wedding reception or rehearsal dinner than a family gathering of 50 people. Likewise, steer clear of the bridal department for items like accessories, fabric and craft supplies that you can usually purchase more economically in another section of the store.

❑ Negotiate, negotiate, negotiate. This rule is as important as the first one about borrowing. Always ask about available discounts. Ordering in quantity, prepaying, paying cash and holding your wedding on a non-peak day are all valid reasons for vendors to give you a price break. Ask and you shall receive.

Wedding Clothes
❑ Save money by wearing your mother's or grandmother's wedding dress or borrowing from a friend. Even if the garment needs to be altered, alterations should still cost less than buying a new dress. Another cheaper alternative to purchasing your dress is to rent it from a bridal shop that does rentals.

❑ If you do decide to purchase your wedding gown, try a bridal outlet or warehouse store rather than shopping at a bridal boutique. These outlets offer substantial discounts on gowns of comparable quality. Check the phone book for bridal outlets in your area.

❑ Accessories can be an expensive add-on when purchased along with your gown. Plan to purchase items such as lingerie, hosiery, your purse and shoes elsewhere.

❑ Make your own veil or headpiece. If you don't feel up to it, ask a friend or relative who sews to do it for you. Look for books on making veils at a library or craft store. Besides saving a great deal of money, your headpiece will hold extra sentimental value because it was made especially for you.

❑ Avoid expensive bridesmaids' gowns. Instead, choose a simple formal that the bridesmaids can actually wear for other occasions. To keep things even simpler, allow bridesmaids to wear dresses they already own that coordinate with your color scheme. Who says your bridesmaid all have to look exactly alike? The same goes for groomsmen. Ask them to wear pants and blazers in a coordinating color such a gray or navy blue that they all probably already own.

❑ Rather than buying a new gown or tuxedo, purchase a used one through the newspaper classifieds. You can also save big by checking consignment stores and thrift stores for used wedding clothes.

❑ Make your own gown or ask a friend or family member who sews to make it for you. If you do go this route, remember the general guideline that everything with the word wedding in it usually costs more. When purchasing fabric, lace, and pearls, check other departments of the fabric store to see if the items you need are sold less expensively than in the bridal department.

❑ Choose a dress that isn't necessarily a wedding dress. An antique white or off-white formal or evening gown will most likely cost less than a gown designed specifically for weddings. The benefit of this is that, unlike a wedding gown, you can wear the dress again later.

❑ To save the expense of renting a tuxedo, the groom can wear his best suit with a new shirt or tie. If he foresees needing a tuxedo in the future, consider buying a used one that can be worn for other occasions. If the groom wants to rent a tuxedo, don't rent his shoes from the tuxedo shop. He probably already has a pair of dark dress shoes that would work. If not, it would be wiser for him to purchase a pair of good quality shoes that he can wear again than to rent.

The Wedding and Reception Sites

❑ Consider having your wedding and reception at home. This saves money both by avoiding a church rental fee and also by limiting the number of people you can invite. If home is not an option, consider other nontraditional sites such as parks, civic centers and other civic sites, which typically have very reasonable rental fees.

❑ Use your own church's facilities. Ask ladies in your church to help out with serving and cleanup in lieu of wedding gifts. The women's groups in some churches may do the catering for a fee as a means of raising money.

❑ In choosing where to have your reception, choose a site that allows you to provide the food yourself or use your own caterer. Some facilities make the majority of their money through their catering, not rental fees, so they require you to use their caterers. This can greatly increase the cost of your reception.

❑ While on the topic of wedding sites, remember that it is customary to give the minister who performs your ceremony some kind of monetary gift for his time and trouble. Do you have an ordained minister in your group of family members and friends? Ask if this person will perform your ceremony as a wedding gift to you.

The Rehearsal Dinner

- ❑ Hold the rehearsal dinner at home, in your church's fellowship hall or in some other place you can use for free. If you don't have access to a free site, think of places such as clubhouses or recreation centers that can be rented inexpensively. These sites may require extra effort to achieve the ambiance you desire, but the savings could be well worth it.

- ❑ Keep the meal casual and uncomplicated. Serve the meal buffet-style with menu items that are conducive to cooking in large quantities such as lasagna, ham, pasta, etc. If you or family members are not up to cooking, buy precooked foods in quantity from a warehouse club or your grocer's deli.

- ❑ Another option is to have the meal catered by a barbecue or chicken restaurant. These restaurants are accustomed to providing cost-efficient meals for large groups and may even throw in extras like napkins, plates and cups, which will save even more.

Reception Food

- ❑ Consider having a potluck reception. Let guests know that you would appreciate their help with the food instead of wedding gifts. This option would work well in close-knit families or church groups where everyone appreciates and supports the bride and groom's desire to celebrate within their means.

- ❑ Choose a simple menu that you can prepare with help from friends and family. Meat and vegetable trays can be purchased from your grocer's deli and then transferred to fancier serving trays. Warehouse clubs such as Sam's and Costco are also a good source of prepackaged foods that can be served in your own decorative dishes.

- ❑ Whether you hire a caterer or do the food yourself, avoid extras and expensive food items that cost more than they are really worth to you. If you do use a catering service, solicit your caterer's help in selecting foods that provide the biggest bang for your buck.

- Have a lunch or mid-afternoon reception that includes lighter, less expensive foods than traditional dinner spreads. Another option is an afternoon tea reception. This kind of reception is typically held between the hours of 2-4pm and features different varieties of tea and finger foods such as sandwiches, fruit and petit fours.
- If you plan to include alcohol, serve only wine and champagne rather than offering a full bar. Also, ask if your caterer will allow you to purchase the liquor yourself from a liquor wholesaler.
- Consider holding your reception at a restaurant with a banquet room. The price the restaurant charges to provide all the food may be less than renting a banquet hall and hiring a caterer.

Invitations

- Consider purchasing cardstock and envelopes from an office supply store or print shop and printing the invitations on your own desktop printer. If you have access to a good quality printer, this is an option worth investigating. Just make sure that the cardstock will go through your printer before purchasing large quantities.
- Instead of a RSVP card with an envelope, save money on postage by using a postcard instead. At the time of this writing, postcard stamps are only 23 cents while first class stamps are 37 cents.
- If you want the elegant look of engraved invitations but don't want to pay the high price, choose thermographed invitations. Thermography is a printing process that simulates the elegance of engraving but is significantly less expensive. If your wedding is informal, consider offset printing for your invitations. This is the cheapest of these three options, but produces a less formal look that is generally not considered appropriate for formal weddings.
- Keep your print order to a minimum. Order just the basic invitations and envelopes. Avoid extras such as thank you notes by purchasing generic note cards or thank you cards

elsewhere. Instead of ordering a separate reception card, put all the reception information on the invitation. Not only will this save on printing, but you will also save on postage. Remember that each additional item you put into the invitation envelope increases the likelihood of paying additional postage.

❑ Are you skilled at calligraphy or do you know someone who is? If your wedding is a small affair, consider handwriting the invitations on cardstock purchased from an office supply store.

Wedding Rings

❑ Select a stone other than a diamond for the engagement ring. Choose an affordable gemstone that has special significance such as your fiancé's birthstone. Another economical option is to choose silver rather than gold for your rings.

❑ Use a family heirloom such as your great grandmother's engagement ring or grandfather's wedding band rather than purchasing a new one. Or check antique stores for antique rings.

❑ If you have a dental technician in the family, he probably knows something about jewelry making. The processes of making jewelry and making dental prosthetics are very similar. He may be able to make your wedding bands for the price of the gold.

❑ Check the newspaper classifieds for used wedding and engagement rings. You can often find bargains resulting from divorce or wedding plans that fell through. Buying from a pawnshop is another option, although some may find the idea of shopping for their wedding rings in a pawnshop unappealing.

Flowers

❑ If you know someone who is a floral designer, ask if she will do the floral arrangements if you provide the flowers. Look for a floral wholesaler in your area that will sell to the public, or use silk flowers for further savings.

❑ Choose multifunctional arrangements that can easily be moved from the chapel or wedding site to the reception hall. After the ceremony, get maximum use out of the bride's and bridesmaids' bouquets by using them to decorate the gift or guest book table.

❑ Spend the majority of your floral budget on arrangements and decorations that have high visibility. Use ribbons and bows, greenery or even balloons for low-visibility areas. Although the temptation is to spend most of floral budget decorating the church, consider spending more on flowers for the reception since that is where guests will spend a majority of their time.

❑ Ask your florist about regional and seasonal flowers. These can be a great deal less expensive than traditional wedding flowers. Ask your florist to help you choose from the most economical varieties available during that time of the year.

❑ Keep bouquets and arrangements simple. Carry a single flower or a small hand-tied bouquet. Another option is for the bride to carry a small bouquet and the bridesmaids to carry single flowers.

❑ Choose a florist that does not charge a consultation fee. A florist should be willing to sit down with you to discuss your needs without charging a fee.

Photography and Videography

❑ Have a professional photographer for the wedding ceremony only. Ask a camera buff friend or relative to take casual pictures at the reception. The same goes for the wedding video if you choose to have one. Hire a videographer for the ceremony only and ask someone else to video the reception with her camcorder.

❑ Another idea for getting a wide variety of casual shots inexpensively is to purchase disposable cameras to place on the tables at the reception. Guests will enjoy using them to take pictures of the happy couple and other guests.

❑ Contact the photography department of your local college to inquire about students who may be available to photograph your wedding for a very reasonable price in order to gain experience.

❑ Buy only what you need. Don't buy a large portrait package from your professional photographer if it contains many more photos than you actually want. Figure out exactly how many pictures you will need for parents, grandparents, friends and yourself. You may find that buying the pictures you want individually is less expensive than the package deals.

The Wedding Cake and Groom's Cake

❑ Ask a friend to make the wedding and groom's cakes for you or make them yourself. If you don't feel confident doing the decorating, do only the baking. Get an experienced friend or relative to ice and decorate the cakes you baked. Another fun idea is to let the groom bake and decorate his own groom's cake.

❑ Rather than a large wedding cake, have only a small professionally decorated wedding cake. Supplement this with white sheet cakes you make and decorate yourself.

❑ If the tradition of saving the top layer of the wedding cake for your first anniversary means nothing to you, plan to use this layer to feed guests so you can order a smaller, less expensive cake.

Music

❑ Hiring a disk jockey is almost always cheaper than using a live band. To keep things even cheaper, record the music you want ahead of time and play it at the reception. Ask a friend to be in charge of keeping the music going.

❑ Contact the music department of your local college to inquire about student musicians who will perform at your wedding for a very reasonable price in order to gain experience.

❑ If you must have live music, choose a smaller group rather than one with several musicians. Generally, the more group members a band has, the higher the charge for hiring them. Consider using just a pianist or guitarist and a vocalist, or a pianist or guitarist who does vocals.

Honeymoon

❑ Lodging is a major honeymoon expense. Brainstorm with your fiancé to come up with ideas for places you can stay free or very inexpensively. Stay in a friend's cabin or beach house. Is someone you know going away for a long vacation? Ask if you can stay in that person's home while enjoying tourist attractions in the area.

❑ If you are adventurous, spend your honeymoon tent camping or rent a cabin in a state park. Another camping option is to borrow or rent a RV or pop-up camper. The advantage of this option is that you can spend a few days in one park and then move on to another area to stay a few days there.

❑ If your honeymoon budget is tight, take a short trip to a destination close by. Then enjoy the rest of your honeymoon at home doing things in your own city that you normally wouldn't have time to do.

❑ If the honeymoon is more important to you than the actual ceremony, plan to spend your money accordingly. Keep expenses for your ceremony to the bare minimum and use the majority of your wedding budget for the honeymoon trip.

Simple and Low-Cost Wedding Gift Ideas

Let's face it. Weddings can be an expensive proposition for everyone—the bride and groom, their parents and all of the guests who purchase gifts for the happy couple. Unfortunately, many of the typical wedding gifts are beautiful but not very practical. Because these items are not things the couple can put to use immediately, the gifts are usually stored on a shelf or in a closet only to be forgotten within a few months. What a shame that what was meant to be a token of the giver's well wishes soon becomes clutter in the couple's new home.

The other common destiny for extravagant yet impractical wedding gifts is the couple's next yard sale. Although some may feel it is gauche to sell wedding gifts, sometimes this is the most practical route for the couple to take. At least that way they get something they can truly use, even if it is only pennies on the dollar of what the giver originally spent.

I believe that many times, givers of wedding gifts get caught up in romantic and fanciful aspects of the special occasion. Hence, they feel that something as commonplace and seemingly humdrum as dishtowels or a doormat is inappropriate. I totally disagree. Wouldn't it be better to give the bride and groom something they can put to use immediately rather than a gift they simply store away?

Below is a list of practical gift ideas for newlyweds. The focus of these gift possibilities is high usability with a low potential for creating clutter. While some of these gift ideas are less expensive than others, they all address legitimate needs of the new couple.

- ❏ Gift certificates from home improvement centers or discount stores for buying things they need around the house that they didn't receive as wedding gifts
- ❏ Gift certificates from restaurants or theaters to be used during the honeymoon or in the months that follow when money may be tight
- ❏ Gift basket filled with common items that every household needs: basic tools, cleaning products, kitchen necessities such as dish towels and sponges, potholders, useful kitchenware such as spatulas, soup ladle, potato peeler, etc.
- ❏ Prepaid phone cards for use on the honeymoon or for calling faraway friends and relatives who couldn't make it to the wedding
- ❏ Grocery store gift certificates for buying all of those little things needed to stock a kitchen for the first time
- ❏ Book of entertainment coupons so they can afford to continue the fun of dating after they are married

❏ Picture frames and albums for displaying all those wedding and honeymoon photos

❏ Film for taking pictures on the honeymoon or during those exciting first months of marriage

❏ Bath towels, hand towels and washcloths—something no new home can be without

❏ Mop bucket with a mop, broom and dustpan—more things every couple needs but doesn't necessarily receive as gifts

❏ Laundry basket or hamper filled with laundry products – If you know the bride and groom will live in an apartment and use a co-op laundry for a while, throw in a roll of quarters.

Giving Wedding Gifts of Your Time

In the chapter on meaningful gift giving, we talked about the art of giving the gift of your time. Now let's look at how this concept of spending time rather than money can be adapted for wedding gift giving.

In the lists of ideas for saving on wedding expenses, a reoccurring suggestion is for the couple to ask friends or relatives to perform services for them. From the perspective of a wedding guest, giving the gift of your time is an excellent way to simplify what can be the stressful and expensive endeavor of finding just the right gift. It is also a wonderful way to relieve some of the stress and expense of wedding planning for the bride and groom.

Instead of buying some gift or gadget the couple may not need, why not look for ways you can do something for the couple that they will remember for a lifetime? When you perform a service for which the couple would otherwise have to pay, you save them money they could use on their honeymoon or in establishing their home. When you volunteer to take care of one facet of wedding or reception preparations, you give the couple the blessing of having one less task to worry about.

Wedding gifts of time fall into three basic categories. The first category includes services related to the wedding that you perform without charge. This kind of gift usually involves a special skill or talent you have. If you decorate cakes, you could volunteer to make the groom's cake or wedding cake. You could sing or play the piano as part of the ceremony. Why not offer to do the floral arrangements or make the corsages and boutonnieres? If you have a flair for doing hair and nails, provide hairstyling and manicures for the bridal party.

Another variety of wedding gifts of time is when you offer to take care of a time-consuming detail that must be done. An example of this is volunteering to address the invitations or cook for the rehearsal dinner. Why not offer to serve at the reception and then organize the cleanup afterward? If the happy couple will be away for several days on their honeymoon, you could watch after their home and take care of pets while they are gone.

One last variation of gifts that involve more time than money is when you use your talents to create a unique keepsake in honor of the couple's special day. If you are musically inclined, you could write a song for the bride and groom. If you paint, give a portrait of the couple as your gift. Write a special poem if you are a poet, or make a quilt if you're a quilter. Such a gift would probably not cost much to create but would be priceless to the recipients.

> Instead of buying some expensive gift or gadget the couple may not need, why not look for ways you can do something for the couple that they will remember for a lifetime?

If you choose to give a gift of time rather than purchasing something, here are a few guidelines to remember. First, if you'd like to provide a service for the wedding, it is best to discuss your idea with the couple soon after they announce their engagement. Most couples begin preparations many months in advance. Knowing about your offer to make the cake or sing in the ceremony will help them as they plan and budget for wedding expenses.

When you present your offer, be sure to do it in such a way that the bride and groom feel confident they can decline without hurting your feelings. Tell them that you want to help out by doing such-and-such as your gift, but if they've already made plans to have that done, you will gladly give or do something else. In talking with the couple, you may be able to identify some other task or service you could perform that would be just as meaningful to them.

Most importantly, remember the couple's wedding day is a once in a lifetime event for them. Do not commit to any sort of gift of time unless you are absolutely certain you can do a good job in fulfilling your promise. If the bride and groom trust you and you let them down on their special day, hard feelings will undoubtedly result. Your gift would be more of a curse than a blessing if not done to the couple's expectations.

Finally, you may also choose to give a small token gift in addition to the gift of your time, especially if you plan to attend a bridal shower in the couple's honor. In most cases, if you are providing a service that saves the couple a great deal of time or money, they will not expect anything else from you. Use your discretion in deciding whether or not to give something inexpensive to supplement your main gift.

Chapter Seven:
Halloween Scaled Down

*A*s a child, I remember Halloween being my favorite holiday next to Christmas. I loved dressing up, going door to door, and at the end of the night, sorting and re-sorting my windfall of goodies. Although we occasionally heard stories of tainted candy or razor blades in apples, my parents were not too concerned. As long as my sister and I stayed in our neighborhood with either my mom or dad trailing behind, we all felt safe to enjoy Halloween as a fun and exciting festivity.

But as Bob Dylan sang, the times they are a-changin'. Just in my 36 years of life, I've seen the number of trick-or-treaters dwindle and the frequency of dangerous incidents increase each year. People aren't as comfortable as they used to be with the idea of sending their children out at night to interact with strangers. Church parties and trick-or-treating in malls are becoming more the norm than the exception. Each year, I wonder how much longer the trick-or-treat tradition will continue.

Although practically everyone I know seems to be more careful and restrictive about Halloween, I find it ironic that this cautious attitude doesn't appear to have hurt Halloween candy sales at all. The National Confectioners Association still ranks Halloween as the most profitable time of the year for candy sellers, even more profitable than Christmas, Easter or Valentine's Day. This organization estimates that 85 percent of American households still hand out candy on the night of October 31st.

In addition to the increase in safety concerns, the attitude toward the holiday has also changed. Fall festivals have replaced Halloween parties as many Christians take a stand against Halloween for religious reasons. Throughout my childhood, no one ever thought twice about decorating with pictures of witches and crystal balls. Now Christians are more aware of the spirit realm and are more vocal in expressing concern over the role the occult plays in traditional Halloween themes.

Are Halloween celebrations a cause for concern? Should trick-or-treating continue as society becomes less safe and more violent? Is Halloween harmless or harmful? These are questions you must answer for yourself, but in order to do so, a look at Halloween history is in order.

The National Confectioners Association still ranks Halloween as the most profitable time of the year for candy sellers, even more profitable than Christmas, Easter or Valentine's Day.

A Bit of Halloween History

Most of the Halloween traditions we see today are dated back to the Celtic tradition of celebrating Samhain (pronounced *sow-en*), the Celtic New Year. The Celtic New Year began on November 1st; therefore, Samhain celebrated both the coming of the New Year and also the beginning of winter.

The Celts believed that during the Samhain festival the night before the New Year, spirits of the dead were free to roam the earth. Tradition held that these spirits were looking for bodies to possess. To frighten the spirits away, people dressed up in scary costumes and lit bonfires. Celtic villagers would go door to door collecting wood for a large communal bonfire and also food offerings to sacrifice to the gods.

Throughout history, it has been a common practice for the Catholic Church to take pagan holidays and give them Christian meaning. In Chapter Three: *Saint Valentine's Day Simplified*, we learned that this is why Saint Valentine's Day was created. The festivities of October 31st took on religious significance around

740AD when Pope Gregory III moved the celebration for all Christian martyrs from May 13th to November 1st. The day was called All Hallows' Day because hallow means holy person. Thus, the night before All Hallows' Day was called All Hallows' Even. Over time, this was shortened to Halloween.

Modern Halloween traditions have roots in cultures other than that of the Celtic people of Ireland. When the Romans conquered the Celts, they adopted the Samhain traditions and mingled them with their own pagan celebrations. The role of apples in modern Halloween festivities—bobbing for apples, giving apples to trick-or-treaters, drinking apple cider—most likely started with Roman festivals honoring the goddess of fruit and orchards.

Besides the Celtic ritual of going from home to home, the tradition of trick-or-treating also has roots in the medieval celebration of All Souls Day. This holiday occurred on November 2nd and was a day set aside to pray for souls of the dead thought to be in purgatory. At this time, children would go from house to house begging for little cakes called soul cakes. In return for the cakes, children had to say a prayer for the givers' deceased relatives. This practice was called souling.

Irish immigrants most likely brought the tradition of pumpkin carving to America. In their home country, people carved out turnips and placed either a candle or ember inside. These early jack-o'-lanterns were used to ward off spirits and represent the souls of deceased family members. When the Irish immigrants came to America, they found that pumpkins were much easier to carve than turnips, so carved pumpkins became a popular Halloween decoration.

The Controversy for Christians

Whether you believe that October 31st celebrations are just good clean fun or something to be avoided at all cost, let's take a moment to examine the controversy for many Christians. Even if you don't agree with these concerns, it is beneficial to understand them nonetheless.

Probably the biggest stumbling block is that Halloween seems to glorify several activities the Bible strictly forbids:

witchcraft, sorcery, divination and fortune telling. In addition, witches, demons and even the Devil himself are portrayed as benign. Many Christians find this troubling. How can parents teach their children that these activities are sinful when they seem perfectly acceptable for Halloween?

> Even if you don't agree with their concerns, it is beneficial to understand the objections many Christians have toward Halloween.

Another argument is that because the holiday has pagan roots, Christians should avoid any connection with it. The Bible teaches followers to avoid appearances of evil (I Thessalonians 5:22) and not to imitate what is evil (3 John 11). It is important to keep in mind, though, that most of our holidays, not just Halloween, began as pagan celebrations that were Christianized over time.

A third argument against Halloween is that the day is a prime time of celebration for occultists and Satanists. Even if we celebrate with fall festivals rather than traditional ghoulish activities, many Christians feel we are still giving credence to Satan's holiday. These people contend that no matter how October 31st is celebrated, there is no such thing as innocent fun on a day that is used for honoring gods other than the God of the Bible.

Additionally, many Christian parents fear that Halloween's emphasis on darkness, ghosts and monsters is not healthy for children. As society becomes more violent, Halloween costumes and decorations have also become more graphic. All this emphasis on blood and gore can be disturbing to small children who aren't able to clearly distinguish fantasy from reality. Even for older children, parents wonder how such a morbid fascination could possibly be positive.

Creative Alternatives to Traditional Halloween Celebrations

Certainly the easiest way to simplify the Halloween celebration is to avoid it altogether, which is what many people do either for religious reasons or simply because the holiday holds no appeal for them. But maybe you're not ready to totally discard this holiday if it held special meaning for you as a child. Perhaps you just want to find a way to celebrate that is simpler or more in keeping with your values and convictions. Either way, here are some ideas for creative alternatives to traditional forms of Halloween celebrations.

- ❏ Make the tradition of dressing up educational by requiring children to dress up as historical or biblical characters. Children will learn as they research their own chosen character and also as they try to guess the identity of other children's characters.

- ❏ Make Halloween a time of giving rather than just receiving for your family. Celebrate Halloween by passing out candy, fruit, or homemade cookies at an orphanage, nursing home or retirement community. Call ahead to schedule your visit and also to ask what treats are best for residents who are on restricted diets. This could also be done in your neighborhood with your children going door to door to give out treats they've made for the neighbors.

- ❏ Use the trick-or-treating time to collect donations for charity. The UNICEF organization sponsors a yearly *Trick-or-Treat for UNICEF* donation drive. See the Halloween section in Chapter Eleven: *Resources* for the website address. You could also collect canned goods for the local food bank or old glasses for an organization that distributes them to the needy.

- ❏ If you are concerned about children eating too many sweets around Halloween, give healthy treats instead of candy. Individual packs of raisins, beef jerky, trail mix, and peanuts are all healthier alternatives. And don't forget about the possibility of giving nonfood treats such as stickers, pencils, crayons, erasers, etc. These items are practical and parents will appreciate the fact that they don't cause tooth decay.

❑ Keep all your celebrations within a Christian theme. Carve Christian symbols or messages on your pumpkin. Hand out biblical comic books with your candy or give fun items that convey a spiritual message. Instead of scary music playing on your porch, greet trick-or-treaters with the sounds of Christian music. Another variation would be to use a patriotic theme.

❑ Make the evening memorable by doing some other activity together as a family instead of trick-or-treating. Take the family out to eat or get together with another family for a pizza party. Go to a movie together, or rent a family favorite and pop some popcorn at home. Have an open house and invite friends to stop by throughout the evening for snacks and fellowship.

❑ Use the Halloween occasion as a group project for reaching out to the community. Rather than a haunted house, work with your church or youth group to set up a heavenly house with angels, biblical characters and skits with a spiritual message. Or host a carnival to provide a safe Halloween alternative for families in the community.

Homemade Costume Ideas

After candy sales, probably the next biggest Halloween moneymaker is the sale of costumes. When you think about it, buying costumes for children is rather silly. Most times a child either outgrows the costume by the next year or no longer wants to be a Teenage Mutant Ninja Turtle or a Teletubby. If costumes are part of your holiday celebration, creating the costumes at home is not only economical, but also offers the greatest opportunity for kids to express their creativity.

Below you will find a list of homemade costume ideas. All of these costumes require only basic supplies you probably already have around the home or can obtain inexpensively. At the end of the list are some basic tried-and-true ideas for quick, last minute costuming.

❑ Postage Stamp – Decorate a large piece of white poster board to look like a postage stamp. Cut holes for your face and arms to go through. Wear a white shirt and pants. You can also use this same concept to make a "Wanted: Dead or Alive" poster costume.

❑ A Tourist – Wear a Hawaiian shirt and walking shorts. Wear a large hat, a pair of sunglasses, and a camera around your neck. For added effect, stick several maps in your pockets and ask everyone you see, "Which way to the Eiffel Tower?"

❑ A Die – Or, if you have a Halloween partner, go as a pair of dice. Paint a big, square box white. Remove one side from the box so the whole thing can slip over your head. Cut holes in the top and sides for your head and arms to go through. Cut black circles from felt or construction paper and glue them in the appropriate places to make the box look like a die. Use this same concept to make a Rubik's Cube® or Christmas gift costume.

❑ Cellular Phone – This idea is similar to the one above. Use a tall skinny box; cut out one of the ends so that the box fits over your body. Paint the box black. Use construction paper or paint to add the display and keypad. Unlike the die costume in which your head sticks out the top, this box will actually rest on top of your head. Cut a hole so that your face can be seen through and also holes for your arms. Use this same concept to make a TV remote control costume. You can also make a post office mailbox costume if you use a larger box.

❑ A Piece of Pizza – Cut each of two large pieces of poster board into the shape of a pizza slice. Using paint, construction paper or felt, decorate one side of each piece with pizza toppings. Attach two strips of poster board to the top edge of the two slices so that they can be worn over the shoulders like a sandwich board. Use this same concept to make an American flag, dollar bill or Oreo® cookie costume.

❑ A Farmer – Wear overalls, a flannel shirt and a big straw hat. For added effect, carry along a shovel. Use a vegetable basket to hold your candy instead of a pumpkin or candy bag.

❏ Miss America – Dress up in a fancy dress and shoes. Use cardboard, glitter, and sequins to make a tiara. Use a wide ribbon or a long strip of construction paper to make a *Miss America* banner to go across your chest.

❏ A Ladybug – Wear a black sweatshirt and black pants or tights. Use a large circle cut from red poster board and smaller circles cut from black construction paper to make the ladybug's shell. Attach straps to the underside of the shell so that the shell can be worn as you would wear a backpack. Attach black pipe cleaners and pompons to a girl's headband to create antennae. Use this same concept to make a turtle, butterfly or bumblebee costume.

❏ A Bag of Jelly Beans – Cut two leg holes in the bottom of a large clear plastic bag. Wear a white sweat suit. Put your legs through the leg holes and then fill the bag up with small balloons of all different colors. Cut two holes for your arms and then get someone to help you fasten the top of the bag around your shoulders with clear tape or safety pins.

❏ Bunch of Grapes – Wear purple or green sweats. Use small safety pins to attach green or purple balloons all over your clothes. The pins go through the tied-off end of the balloon, near the knot. If you want, wear a brown hat or knit cap to look like the stem.

❏ Pizza delivery person – This one is simple. Just dress like an employee from your local pizza joint. Carry a cardboard pizza box to use instead of a bag for holding your Halloween candy. Instead of saying "Trick or Treat," say "Joe's Pizza!" Use this same concept to make a waitress or maitre d' costume. Instead of a pizza box, carry a serving tray with plastic dinnerware attached.

❏ Faithful standby ideas: clown, scarecrow, old man or woman, princess, cheerleader, angel, nerd, cowboy, ballerina, bride, hobo, any type of athlete, hippie, or any distinguishable profession such as a doctor, fireman, carpenter, nurse, etc.

Remember not to get too worked up over your children's costumes. Most kids love dressing up in any kind of clothes they don't normally wear; the clothes don't have to represent a particular character. Some of the happiest trick-or-treaters I've seen are the ones who say, "I dunno," when asked what their costumes are supposed to be. If you find yourself in need of quick children's costumes, pull out all the outdated clothes, gaudy jewelry, weird hats and bright makeup that you can find and let the kids go for it!

Chapter Eight:
Keeping the Thanksgiving
Celebration Simple

*H*ave you ever wanted to throw a big party to celebrate the accomplishment of some difficult task? Or maybe something wonderful happened and you wanted to call all your friends and neighbors over for a lavish feast to celebrate. This desire to share our joys is a natural reaction when we feel particularly thankful for favorable events in our lives. We experience it today, and the early settlers experienced it at the close of their first year in the New World.

A Bit of Thanksgiving History

Ironically, the event most people consider to be the first Thanksgiving was not actually the first Day of Thanksgiving observed in the New World. The celebration was also probably not in November but most likely in October. Even more surprising, the day was not a true Day of Thanksgiving in the eyes of those who participated.

The earliest settlers believed any favorable circumstances resulted from God's pleasure with them while anything unfavorable resulted from His displeasure. They routinely observed Days of Thanksgiving and Praise, and Days of Fasting and Humiliation as part of their religious observances. These days were spent praying and worshipping at church with a modest meal at home afterward.

The famous harvest celebration the Pilgrims held in 1621 was a one-time event that would have most likely been forgotten if it had not been recorded in a document that was discovered many years later. It wasn't until 1777 that a national day of Thanksgiving was called; even then, the day was a religious holiday to give thanks for a particular favorable event, not a time of feasting like the celebration of 1621. The tradition of celebrating Thanksgiving annually started in 1863 when President Abraham Lincoln declared a national day of Thanksgiving on the last Thursday in November. Every president since then has followed suit.

Following the Pilgrims' Example (Sort of)

The myth of the first Thanksgiving, complete with Pilgrims and Indians, is probably so enduring because the celebration they had more closely resembles Thanksgiving as we know it. Joyous feasting, bountiful food, and fellowship with family and friends are more familiar to us than spending the day praying and listening to sermons at church. And although our celebrations don't last three days like that of the Pilgrims and Wampanoag Indians, many of us do make a weekend of it since the Thursday holiday creates a perfect excuse to take Friday off from work.

Many similarities exist between the Pilgrims' celebration and the way we celebrate today, but there are some differences, too. Although the settlers' celebratory spread was plentiful, I believe it is highly unlikely that any participants overindulged as we often do at our Thanksgiving dinners. Their strict Puritan beliefs would have most certainly prohibited such lack of self-control. Also, since food had been so scarce at times during the Pilgrims' first year, it is doubtful that any leftovers from their spread went to waste. In contrast, how many times do we end up chucking food because we had way too much from the start?

Another difference is the motivation behind the festivities. The Pilgrims celebrated out of a true spirit of gratitude. Only about half of the original Mayflower travelers actually survived the first winter in the New World. Had it not been for the help and guidance of the Wampanoag Indians, many other settlers may have died as well. In addition, the fall crops had done much better than expected. For the Pilgrims, a bountiful harvest celebration was the best way they knew to commemorate their good fortune. Unfortunately, we seem to have lost this focus on true thankfulness. Although each of us has a multitude of reasons to be thankful, we often tend to celebrate the holiday more out of habit than heartfelt gratitude.

How can we infuse our modern Thanksgiving celebrations with the sort of deep appreciation the Pilgrims had? I believe the first step is to realize that the spirit of Thanksgiving shouldn't make only a once a year appearance. Because the settlers regularly observed Days of Thanksgiving, the festival they held in 1621 was probably even more significant because it was a culmination of acts and attitudes they practiced all year long. Maybe this is the key to making our celebrations more meaningful as well.

> Although each of us has a multitude of reasons to be thankful, we often tend to celebrate Thanksgiving more out of habit than heartfelt gratitude.

Celebrate Thanksgiving All Year Long

My favorite Thanksgiving memory is somewhat unique because it didn't occur on Thanksgiving Day or even in November. This special celebration took place in August, only days before I left the country to spend a year in Japan.

My parents weren't thrilled about their youngest daughter moving halfway around the world, but they tried to be supportive. I don't know which bothered them more: the fact that I knew absolutely no one in Japan or that I told them not to expect me home for the holidays. Either way, it was my dear mother who came up with the idea of having a special Thanksgiving meal for me before I left. "They probably won't have turkey dinners in Japan," she said. With that, Mom set out to plan an extraordinary holiday meal.

And extraordinary it was. We had turkey and stuffing, gravy, fresh baked rolls, pumpkin pie and even the sweet potatoes my father and I love. Even though the rest of the family would celebrate again in November, Mom worked hard to make my special Thanksgiving feast the best ever.

Thinking back on that memory, I am reminded of the things that make Thanksgiving so meaningful: festive foods and decorations, time with loved ones, and time for taking inventory of our blessings. This makes me wonder. Why do we usually save these things for Thanksgiving? Why not incorporate a little bit of the holiday into the other months as well?

Festive Foods and Decorations – Have you ever eaten turkey and dressing in April? How about pumpkin pie in February? There's no rule that says you can only eat these foods in November. And why should the fine china and silver stay packed away all year? Add a little holiday magic to any family meal by serving holiday foods or using the dishes you normally save for company. Just think how honored your family will feel when you pull out the linen tablecloth just because.

Time with Loved Ones – A big part of what makes Thanksgiving memorable for me is getting the whole clan together for an afternoon of fellowship. Laughing, talking, telling stories of cute things the children have done—these are the times that add warmth and richness to life. Why not start a monthly or bimonthly tradition of getting all family members together just to catch up on the happenings in their lives? If you don't have family nearby, start this tradition with friends whom you don't see as often as you'd like.

Time for Taking Inventory – Often we allow ourselves to become distracted by the hustle and bustle of our daily lives. One look at the evening news or visit to an intensive care unit provides a powerful reminder of how many reasons we have to be grateful. Thankfulness should not be a ritual reserved only for November. Expressing gratitude and giving thanks are activities that never go out of season.

Ideas for Making Thanksgiving More Meaningful

In addition to spreading the spirit of Thanksgiving throughout the year, another way to further enrich your family celebration is to incorporate meaningful activities into your special day. Here are some ideas for enriching your family's celebration.

❑ Combine holiday decorating with expressions of thankfulness. Use construction paper to make colored leaves, pumpkins and other seasonal symbols. Write down reasons why you feel thankful on each cutout. Use these decorations to give the house a festive look.

❑ Incorporate worship into your Thanksgiving festivities. Follow the Pilgrims' pattern for Days of Thanksgiving and Praise by spending some family time in prayer, singing and scripture reading before enjoying your feast.

❑ Either before the feasting begins or after the meal, go around the table and ask each family member to finish this sentence; "This year I am most thankful for..." To keep it simple for small children, use the sentence starter, "I am thankful because..."

❑ Make the Thanksgiving meal educational by dressing up as Pilgrims and Indians and eating foods similar to the ones they would have eaten. Children will learn a bit of history as you help them research what kinds of clothes were worn and what foods were eaten during that time period.

❑ Invite someone to your family dinner who cannot celebrate Thanksgiving with her own family: an elderly person whose children live far away, a college student who cannot afford to travel, or a member of the armed services who is stationed far from home.

❑ Sending Christmas cards is a common family tradition; why not send Thanksgiving cards as well? Purchase blank greeting cards with a fall theme or make your own. Inside write a note thanking the recipient for something special she has done or the positive impact she has had on your life.

❑ Use the Thanksgiving holiday to remember those who regularly go without enough to eat. Fast or eat very small meals the day before Thanksgiving to remind yourself how it feels to be hungry. Give the money that would have been spent on the day's meals to an organization that feeds the hungry.

❑ Throughout the month of November, read scriptures and other inspirational writings about thankfulness. As a family, talk about what the verses mean and how you can apply them to your lives.

❑ Help someone from a foreign country experience a bit of American culture. Invite the person and his family to celebrate Thanksgiving with your family. Not only will your guests discover more about this country, but your family will also get the opportunity to interact with people from a different culture.

❑ Express your thankfulness by sharing your blessings with the less fortunate. As a family, select a charity to support and devise a plan for how you will give to that organization. For example, have a family yard sale if temperatures permit and give a portion of your profits to the Salvation Army. Or all family members can save some of their allowances each week during November. Use this money to buy groceries to donate to the local food bank.

❑ Create a Blessing Jar or Blessing Basket. Put the basket or jar along with a pencil and pieces of paper in a central place in your home. Throughout November, ask family members to write some of their blessings on the pieces of paper and put them in the container. Read these blessings aloud during your Thanksgiving meal. At the end of the meal, say a prayer of thanks for all the ways in which your family has been blessed.

Feast on These Thanksgiving Savings

Besides adding meaning to your Thanksgiving, you are probably also interested in ways to trim down the cost. If you've ever planned a Thanksgiving feast, you know that the cost of buying all the food and decorations can add up faster than you can say, "Gobble, gobble."

Because it is a special occasion, we tend to think, "Oh, why not splurge a little?" Add this splurge component to the fact that most holiday meals include extra mouths to feed, and before you know it, you've got a major expense on your hands. Here are some practical ideas for saving money on your holiday celebration.

❑ Serve ham or turkey, but not both. Choose one meat or main dish and plan the rest of your meal around it. This not only saves the cost of the additional meat, but also the cost of special side dishes that go with it. The cost of electricity for cooking both meats is reduced, too.

❑ Go potluck. If it isn't already a tradition in your family, make Thanksgiving dinner a potluck meal. Why should one person do all the work and bear all the expense? Besides, everyone will have fun tasting favorite recipes of several different cooks.

❑ Balance expensive and cheap dishes. Mashed potatoes are less expensive to make than a creamy vegetable casserole; a pumpkin pie is generally cheaper to make than a homemade cheesecake. Limit the number of dishes requiring expensive ingredients. Choose your family's favorites and serve inexpensive dishes to complement them.

❑ Trim down extras. Do you really need four different vegetables and three different desserts? Usually there is too much food at Thanksgiving dinners anyway. Who will miss that extra casserole or choice of bread? Try to cut out at least one extra that no one will miss from each food category.

❑ Serve inexpensive beverages. Sodas and fruit juices can be expensive add-ons to your Thanksgiving shopping list.

Water, coffee (approximately .03¢ per 8oz serving), tea (.04¢ per serving) and Kool-Aid® (.06¢ per serving) are very economical beverage choices. Soda and juice generally cost between 11¢ - 37¢ or more per serving.

❑ Dispose of disposables. Disposable plates, cups, napkins and utensils are an added expense to your holiday meal, especially if you buy the decorative variety. Carefully consider if the convenience is worth the extra expense. If everyone pitches in, doing the dishes might not be so bad after all.

❑ Maximize oven use. Try to do as much of your baking at one time as possible to cut down on electricity use. Conserve electricity also by using the microwave oven whenever possible.

❑ Decorate naturally. Use natural decorations such as dried autumn leaves and pinecones. Fall fruits and vegetables, acorns, and tiny pumpkins also add a festive look. Look in magazines for ideas; then adapt those decorating ideas using things you have on hand. With some advanced planning, you can even grow your own pumpkins and winter squash for the occasion.

❑ Watch those giveaways. Grocery stores often run promotions in which they give away turkeys with the purchase of other items such as hams. Don't let the idea of getting something free cause you to cook a bigger meal than you actually need. That free turkey is not really free when you factor in the extra items you bought to go with the ham you didn't originally plan to purchase.

❑ Plan in advance. Decide on your menu and make your shopping list several weeks in advance. Then watch for sales on those items you need. Remember the old saying, "Haste makes waste"? You'll probably spend more when you buy at the last minute.

❑ Take advantage of loss leaders. In the weeks before Thanksgiving, grocery stores run fantastic specials on traditional holiday foods. They hope that while visiting their stores to get the specials, you'll also buy a shopping cart full of other things. Be a savvy shopper. Take advantage of each store's specials without falling into the extra spending trap.

❑ Look for substitutions. Many holiday recipes call for ingredients you don't normally keep on hand. Before buying special ingredients you'll only use once, check the substitution guides in your cookbooks to see if there is anything you can substitute. For example, 1 cup minus 2 tablespoons of all-purpose flour can be substituted for 1 cup of cake flour; 1 cup of sugar plus 1/4 cup of liquid can be substituted for 1 cup of honey or corn syrup.

❑ Fresh is not necessarily best. Experts say there is no real difference in taste between a fresh and frozen turkey. It's all a matter of preference and convenience. Therefore, watch for sales and go with whatever is cheapest.

❑ Don't waste. Stored in the refrigerator, cooked turkey should be eaten within 3-4 days. Kept in the freezer, it is good for up to 6 months. Be realistic about how many leftovers your family can eat in the days after Thanksgiving. Freeze the extras right away so you won't end up chucking them.

❑ Choose the right size bird. The turkey experts at Honeysuckle White recommend an 8-12 pound turkey for 2-4 people; a 12-16 pound turkey for 4-6 people; a 14-18 pound turkey for 6-8 people; an 18-20 pound turkey for 8-10 people; and a 20-24 pound turkey for 11-13 guests. These estimates allow for some leftovers. If your family doesn't like leftovers, nip the problem of wasted leftovers in the bud by choosing a turkey on the low end of the suggested weight range.

❑ Love those leftovers. Some of the greatest Thanksgiving savings occur after the holiday if you know how to put your leftovers to good use. However, a family can only be expected to eat so many turkey sandwiches. Look for interesting new recipes to give that leftover turkey a lift.

Hospitality versus Entertaining

Because the Thanksgiving holiday often includes inviting friends and relatives to share your celebration, this is a good time to talk about hospitality. Although this topic also applies to other special occasions, we'll use the Thanksgiving celebration to illustrate the significant difference between entertaining and extending hospitality.

For most people, the main focus at Thanksgiving is food and fellowship at home, either your own home or someone else's.

> Think of it this way: Entertaining makes you look good, but extending hospitality makes your guests feel good.

Several years ago, a coworker shared a profound secret with me about this act of having guests in your home. I'll never forget what she said. It was so simple, yet so powerful: "When you entertain, you bring honor and glory to yourself. Showing hospitality brings honor and glory to God." Stated another way, entertaining makes you look good but extending hospitality makes your guests feel good.

Think about it. Pride can easily sneak in when you entertain. The meal you serve shows off *your* cooking abilities. Everything is clean and neat so guests are impressed with *your* home and homemaking skills. And, if the gathering is enjoyable, everyone assumes it is due to *your* talents as a host. Why, all this focus on yourself can lead to an inflated ego if you're not careful!

Hospitality, on the other hand, is not about impressing anyone. It's about being yourself and making your guests feel comfortable to be themselves. It doesn't matter whether you serve frozen pizza or if your house wouldn't pass the white glove test. Through your warmth and humility, guests feel closer to you and better about themselves for having been there.

Do you have special friends whose home you love to visit? Is it because they serve 10-course meals on their finest china or because every corner of their house is spotless? Of course not. Neither extravagance nor perfection is what makes a visit enjoyable. Warm hospitality is what turns an ordinary get-together into a memorable occasion. When you feel love and acceptance extended to you through your hosts, you can't help but want to come again.

Certainly there is a time and a place for entertaining, like when important business clients are in from out of town. But how often does that happen? Most guests in your home don't come there expecting to be impressed. They would much rather be treated like family.

Entertaining can be a major cause of stress during any holiday or special occasion. If the thought of trying to host picture-perfect social gatherings is a big worry for you, why not try showing hospitality instead? Forget about dazzling your guests with all the wonderful things you can do. Try instead to make your guests feel at home as you relax, be yourself, and forget about the white glove test!

Tips for the Hospitality Challenged

This notion of showing hospitality sounds simple enough, but some people still feel insecure about inviting others into their homes. Even with the pressure to entertain removed, the thought of planning, organizing, and cooking for such a gathering can be overwhelming.

If this describes your feelings exactly, please remember that we all have different gifts and abilities. What comes easily for one person can be a genuine source of anxiety and apprehension for another. Yet, practically all of us encounter times when we feel called to be a blessing to someone else by showing hospitality. If you feel that hospitality is not your forte, here are tips for making the task a little easier to undertake.

- ❏ Ask for help. If you are nervous about an upcoming visit from guests, talk to someone about it. Solicit suggestions for easy meals, engaging activities or interesting topics of conversation. If you have a close friend who is a whiz at organizing such events, ask her to come over and help with preparations. Likewise, if you have a friend who is naturally the life of the party, why not invite her to the gathering to help keep the evening lively?

❑ Another way to lighten the load is to make the gathering a potluck. Ask guests to bring their favorite appetizers or desserts. If you are uncomfortable with making such a request, an easy way to do this is to have a few items in mind just in case guests ask if there is anything they can bring.

❑ Keep things simple. Instead of a meat, two veggies, bread and dessert, would one main dish that contains vegetables, along with a dessert work just as well? Instead of a whole meal, would finger foods suffice? Lessen your stress by lessening the number of necessary preparations.

❑ Stick with foods you are comfortable cooking and serving. Trying a fancy new recipe on an occasion when you already feel uneasy is a recipe for disaster! The same goes for activities you plan. If you are not sure how well something will work, you should probably save it for another time.

❑ Watch and learn from someone whose hospitality skills you admire. What little things does she do to make everything go more smoothly? Don't be afraid to ask that person to share with you what she has learned from experience.

❑ Give yourself a break. Don't put yourself on a guilt trip because the gift of showing hospitality doesn't come naturally to you. Try not to compare yourself to others. Allowing yourself to engage in this kind of thinking is self-defeating. Just do the best you can and forget about what someone else would or could do.

Chapter Nine:
Celebrating Birthdays and
Anniversaries Simply

*B*irthdays and anniversaries are essentially celebrations of the same thing: the number of years of living the person or couple has enjoyed. Unlike Christmas and Valentine's Day, which fall on the same day for everyone who celebrates, birthdays and anniversaries are unique to the individual. These special occasions are like your own personal holidays that you can celebrate any way you wish.

Whether you choose to celebrate or not, birthdays and anniversaries do perform an important function in our culture. Birthdays reinforce the value of each individual. These celebrations commemorate the day the honoree became a part of the family unit and the value he brings to it. In the same way, anniversaries memorialize the sacred merging of two distinct lives into one new life together. Anniversary celebrations give us an opportunity to honor the husband and wife for their endurance and faithfulness to the commitment they made to each other.

The History of Birthday Partying

We know the tradition of celebrating birthdays with special festivities dates back at least as far as Bible times because there are two examples of birthday parties in the Bible. One is in the Old Testament in Genesis chapter 40. In the story of Joseph, we are told that the ruling Pharaoh celebrated his birthday by giving a big feast for his officials. During this party, Joseph's interpretations of dreams came true: Pharaoh reinstated the butler to his old job and ordered the baker to be hung by a noose.

The other example of a biblical birthday party is found in the story of John the Baptist (Mark 6). In this story, King Herod held a big feast to celebrate his own birthday and invited all the high officials and military commanders. At this birthday party,

Herodias' daughter strutted her stuff, Herod ran his big mouth, and a few hours later, John the Baptist's head ended up on a platter.

The fact that we only have record of kings celebrating their birthdays in the Bible is par for the course in other accounts of ancient history as well. We know that ancient people numbered their years of life for as long as the calendar existed, but it appears that birthday celebrations were only for rulers and other important people. Maybe this was because birthdays were celebrated with lavish parties that common people could not afford. Even if average people did celebrate their birthdays on a simpler scale, these events are unknown because they were not recorded. Ancient historians recorded only the birthday celebrations of people of prominence such as kings, leaders and nobility.

> If not handled with care, the whole birthday scenario presents the perfect breeding ground for the "Gimmes" and the "I wants."

The Makings of a Birthday Monster

Although most people today don't throw extravagant birthday parties for themselves, our cultural norms for celebrating birthdays present some challenges, especially with children. So much emphasis on catering to the birthday child's every whim can encourage an attitude of selfishness and greed. At least at Christmas, everyone receives presents, but at one's birthday, he is the center of attention. If not handled carefully, this scenario presents the perfect breeding ground for the "Gimmes" and the "I wants." If a child sees his parents spending more than they can afford to indulge him on his birthday, the young person may come to believe that spending above his means is acceptable.

Another challenge is that parents often feel they have to spend a lot to make their children's parties a success. Some parents feel a sort of peer pressure to keep up with friends and neighbors. If the child's classmates are having expensive birthday bashes at the hot new high-tech arcade, parents may resort to going with the flow so their child won't feel deprived. Doing so not only teaches children that they must keep up with their peers, but it also deprives them of the wonderful opportunity to use their creativity to come up with something unique and more enjoyable than what everyone else is doing.

Birthday Traditions That Take the Emphasis Off of Self

There is nothing wrong with making family members feel loved and appreciated on their birthdays. As we said earlier, birthdays serve the important function of reaffirming one's sense of belonging and value to the family unit. The key is to celebrate in ways that convey the birthday person's significance within the context of the family.

Instead of doing the usual birthday celebrations each year, why not start some new birthday traditions? Below are ideas for both children and adults that honor the birthday person without putting an inordinate emphasis on self and selfish indulgences.

❑ Your birthday is not only significant to you, but the day you were born was also a momentous occasion for the one who gave birth to you. Use your birthday as an excuse to do something special for your mother to show appreciation to her for bringing you into the world.

❑ Rather than gifts and parties, make it a tradition to celebrate family birthdays by treating the birthday person to a day off from chores and responsibilities. Add to the excitement by allowing her to select the family menu and activities for the whole day. Although the honoree is still the center of attention, she is made to feel special in ways that don't involve spending.

❑ Make the birthday party a time of giving, not just receiving. Party guests usually bring gifts for the birthday person. Why shouldn't the birthday person also give gifts to the special friends who help celebrate his birthday? Instead of buying favors or gifts, the child could make craft items to give to guests. The birthday child could also help make homemade cookies or candy to fill goodie bags. If the child is celebrating his birthday with his class at school, he may choose to give one gift everyone in the class can enjoy such as a new board game or a book for the teacher to read aloud.

❑ Another twist on the idea of everyone getting a gift is to ask each guest to bring a small wrapped toy or inexpensive gift item from home that they are no longer using. These presents are then used for a gift swap during the party so that everyone gets to share in the fun of receiving and opening gifts.

❑ Make it a tradition to give a gift to charity in honor of the birthday person. This could be in lieu of a birthday gift or in addition to a modest gift. Let the honoree choose which charity will receive the gift in her honor.

❑ Instead of having a large party, allow the honoree to select a special outing to experience. Depending on how much is budgeted, this could be something as simple as going to see a movie or something more elaborate like a hot air balloon ride. Allow the child to choose one or two close friends with whom to share the experience. This could also be done with the birthday person choosing one special experience for the whole family to enjoy together.

❑ To take the emphasis off of material possessions, ask party guests not to bring gifts, but rather to give IOUs for things they will do for or with the honoree. For example, "I owe you a Saturday afternoon picnic in the park," or "I owe you help with your next home repair project."

❑ Instead of or in addition to modest gifts, start the tradition of giving birthday blessings. Ask family members and guests to speak words of blessing that they wish for the birthday person throughout the coming year. The spoken word is powerful and can prove to be self-fulfilling. Be sure that this important time during the celebration receives just as much fanfare as gift opening.

Alternative Birthday Celebrations for Kids of All Ages

Earlier we discussed the pressure parents sometimes feel to celebrate their children's birthdays with just as much expense and fanfare as friends or neighbors. Additionally, they may experience stress over trying to throw the latest and greatest theme party when their budgets truly don't allow for such an expense.

What a pity that some parents feel they must spend a great deal for their kids to have a memorable celebration. The material aspects of a gathering are not what make an event unforgettable. Six months from now the child won't remember the details of the food, decorations, or presents, but rather the fun and fellowship shared with guests. Below are some out-of-the-ordinary party ideas for both children and adults that put less emphasis on materialism and more emphasis on the relational aspects of celebrating.

- ❑ An Afternoon Tea Party – This mid-afternoon party offers guests a fun opportunity to dress up and act dignified. The food is simple. You provide finger foods such as fruit, small sandwiches, cookies or pastries, and a variety of flavored teas served in cups with saucers. If the birthday child and friends are too young for tea, serve hot apple cider or lemonade.

- ❑ A Craft Birthday Party – Pick one craft that is appropriate for the age group and that can be completed in one session. Intersperse the steps required to complete the craft with traditional birthday party activities such as opening presents, cutting the cake, etc. Guests go away from the party with knowledge of how to do a new craft and also a piece of their own handiwork.

- ❑ A Potluck Party – The host family provides the main course; everyone else brings side dishes, drinks and desserts. To make this party even more personalized, each guest can prepare and bring one of the honoree's favorite foods.

- ❑ An International Dinner – This party provides a wonderful opportunity for everyone to learn about another culture. Select a particular country and celebrate as the people of that country would. Serve authentic dishes from that country, and for entertainment play games and music of that country. Test guests' knowledge by asking trivia questions about the featured country.

❑ Progressive Dinner – Arrange for the birthday person to celebrate in several different places. Start at one friend's home for appetizers. Then the birthday person and party guests go to someone else's home for soup or salad. The next friend in the progression provides the entrée and the friend at the last home serves dessert. The honoree can open one gift at each home or collect all the gifts to be opened at the last home as the finale of the evening.

❑ A Card Party – This works especially well for older people who have lost touch with friends and neighbors over the years. Without the honoree's knowledge, ask as many friends and relatives as you can contact from around the country to send a birthday greeting or card. If you really want to make things easy for them, send preaddressed, stamped envelopes for them to use. The recipient will be surprised and overjoyed that so many people remembered her special day. Another alternative is to ask friends and family members to send electronic greeting cards to the recipient's email address.

❑ A Homemade Gift Birthday Party – Ask guests to bring something they've made. Just state on the invitation that instead of buying gifts, everyone should bring a handmade gift for the birthday person.

❑ A Yard Sale or Flea Market Party – Rather than going to an arcade or roller rink, take the birthday child and several close friends on a yard sale or flea market shopping trip. Give each guest a small amount of money to spend. Let the items they buy serve as party favors. Follow up with finger foods and birthday cake at home.

❑ Treasure Hunt Party – This works great if you have a large area in which to hide clues. For added fun, make a treasure map that directs the way to each clue. Make the treasure something that can be shared and enjoyed by all the guests. The treasure items can also serve as party favors for guests to take home.

- ❑ Scavenger Hunt Party – This party works better for guests who are old enough to drive. Otherwise, you will need several chaperones to help with the driving. Make a list of offbeat items the guests must find such as a doctor's signature or a map of a neighboring state. Set a time at which everyone must meet back at a central location to see which group collected the most items from the list. Give a prize to the group collecting the most items, and for fun, award a gag prize for the group collecting the least.

- ❑ "Getting Out of Debt" Party – If several couples are working on getting their finances in order, this could be a fun way to use the honoree's birthday as an occasion to encourage each other. Guests dress to indicate how close they are to getting out of debt. Dressing in all red means they have a long way to go; wearing mostly black with only a little red means they're almost debt-free. In keeping with the theme of saving money, gifts should cost less than $5.

- ❑ Homemade Pizza Party – Allow guests to make their own pizzas from scratch, crust and all. To keep things simpler, you can buy premade crusts and provide a variety of toppings. The pizza making serves as a major party activity; the completed pizzas serve as the main course for the meal. Award prizes for the most creative combinations of toppings, the most photogenic pizza, etc.

- ❑ Banana Split Party – Provide a wide assortment of ice cream, bananas and toppings. Let guests make their own sweet treats to go along with the birthday cake.

- ❑ Makeover Birthday Party – Ask as many of the following people as you know to come do their magic on party guests: a hairstylist, makeup artist, skin care consultant, manicurist, etc. If you don't know any professionals who can come, ask guests to bring their own makeup, curling irons and manicure kits to give each other makeovers.

❑ An Educational Birthday Party – Arrange for members of the local fire department to come to your party and give a talk on fire safety. Ask if they can bring the fire engine for the kids to see. Or inquire about having a policeman come out in a squad car to talk to the group about his job.

❑ A Half-Birthday Party – Why should each person have to wait a whole year for a special day? Celebrate half birthdays by making half of a birthday cake. To do this, cut a round layer of cake in half, flip one half over and stack it on top of the other before decorating. At the half-birthday party, serve guests half sandwiches and sing half of the birthday song. This idea could be altered for an adopted child by celebrating the day the adoption was finalized in addition to the actual date of birth.

Make It Yourself Ice Cream Cake

While on the topic of birthday celebrations, let's spend a few moments talking about cakes. Often the birthday cake is the centerpiece of the celebration, especially when the party is a low budget affair. In that case, the parent or organizer of the party may want to make the cake extra special since other aspects of the party are simple.

Ice cream cakes are popular with kids and adults alike. The problem with store-bought cakes, though, is that they can be expensive. Also, if you purchase a pre-made cake, you don't have much choice about what flavors of cake and ice cream are inside. You can preorder custom ice cream cakes at ice cream and yogurt shops, but even so, these cakes usually just include cake and ice cream without any other goodies inside.

Wouldn't it be great if you could make your own ice cream cake and personalize it with all of the birthday person's favorite flavors and toppings? Several years ago a friend shared with me the basics of how to make ice cream cakes at home. Since then, homemade ice cream cake has become a family favorite for birthdays, anniversaries, holidays—any excuse we can possibly use for whipping one up.

The recipe is relatively simple. If you have to go out and buy all the ingredients you want to use, you might end up spending as much as you would for a store-bought cake. However, you can keep the cost down by using ingredients you already have on hand. The beauty of this basic recipe is that you can use whatever you want, whatever would make the cake special for the honoree. Be creative in concocting unique combinations that suit your fancy.

Ingredients You'll Need:

- ❏ 1 - 1½ quarts of ice cream (any flavor) – This is approximate. You may use more or less depending on how generous you are with the ice cream.
- ❏ 1 - 8″ or 9″ layer of cake (any flavor), baked and cooled – Most cake mixes make two layers. Go ahead and bake the second layer. Wrap it tightly and save it in the freezer for the next ice cream cake you make.
- ❏ Tub of whipped topping – Again, exactly how much you'll use depends on how generous you are with it. I love whipped topping so I usually make sure I start with at least a 16oz tub.
- ❏ A variety of toppings to be used in the layering process – You can use chopped nuts, crumbled cookies, chocolate chips, chocolate or peanut butter candy pieces, chocolate or caramel sauce, jam, whipped topping, crumbled graham crackers, fresh fruit, or just about anything you like.

Supplies You'll Need:

- ❏ A bowl – It's best to use one that has deep, straight sides and a fairly flat bottom. The diameter of the bowl should be as close to the size of the layer of cake as possible.
- ❏ Plastic wrap
- ❏ A plate to put the cake on for decorating and serving
- ❏ Spoons and spatulas for scooping and spreading

Preparing Your Bowl:

Start by taking the ice cream out of the freezer to soften to a nice, workable consistency while you prepare the bowl. Place long pieces of plastic wrap across the bowl in a crisscross fashion. Press the wrap down and smooth it along the inside of the bowl. Use enough plastic wrap to have several inches hanging over the top rim of the bowl. Make sure the entire inside surface of the bowl is covered.

Assembly:

1. Start with a layer of ice cream. Scoop softened ice cream into the bowl, completely covering the bottom of the bowl. Use the back of a spoon to smooth it out.
2. Make a layer consisting of some combination of toppings.
3. Add the layer of cake. Press it down firmly. If the diameter of your bowl is bigger than the diameter of the cake, you can press even harder to flatten it to fill the width of the bowl. However, don't worry if the cake doesn't completely fill the width of the bowl. You can press spoonfuls of ice cream down into the gap or camouflage the gap with whipped topping when you ice the cake.
4. Add another layer of toppings.
5. Add another layer of ice cream. Smooth it out with a spoon.
6. If you'd like, add one last layer of toppings such as vanilla wafers or crumbled cookies to serve as a crust on the bottom.

After adding all layers, fold the excess plastic wrap around the top of the bowl down over the last layer of the cake to cover it. Make sure it is completely covered; use more plastic wrap if necessary. Freeze overnight or until hard. To remove the cake from the bowl, dip the bottom of the bowl in warm water for a few seconds. Unfold the long pieces of plastic wrap and use them to pull the cake loose from the bowl.

When the cake is loose enough to remove it from the bowl, fold the plastic wrap down over the outside of the bowl. Hold a plate securely over the bowl and flip it over. The cake should come out onto the plate. If it doesn't, dip the bowl in the warm water again. Remove the plastic wrap from the cake and discard.

Use whipped topping to frost the cake. Decorate as desired. If the ice cream starts to melt at any time while you are decorating, put the cake back in the freezer for several minutes to harden. When you finish decorating the cake, store it in the freezer until party time.

As I said, homemade ice cream cake is very popular in our family. A typical Twigg family cake usually consists of a layer of neapolitan ice cream, chocolate sauce, crumbled cookies, whipped topping, a layer of chocolate cake, strawberry jam, more ice cream, more chocolate sauce and crumbled chocolate graham crackers on the bottom. Delicious!

Saving Money on Kids' Birthday Parties

If you do decide to go the traditional route for your child's birthday party, consider these ideas for cutting the cost of the celebration.

- ❑ Plan activities that are multifunctional. For example, plan a craft for each guest to make; this serves as both a party activity and party favor. Providing all the fixings and allowing guests to make individual pizzas or sub sandwiches serves as an activity and takes care of part of the party food.
- ❑ Use photos as party favors. If you have a clown come to entertain, take Polaroid pictures of each guest with the clown. If the birthday girl has a makeover party, take before and after pictures of each guest. Slide photos into inexpensive paper frames to serve as the party favors. A cheaper alternative to taking Polaroid pictures is to use a digital camera. However, this option requires a helper who can sneak away to the computer and print out the pictures before the party is over.
- ❑ Watch store clearance tables for items that can be used for birthday parties in the months following a holiday. Candy, colorful gift bags and small novelty items can be used as party favors. Watch for decorations you could use such as streamers and balloons as well as colored napkins, cups and plates.

❑ If you're not up to making the ice cream cake we talked about earlier and you know someone who decorates cakes, ask if that person will make the birthday cake for you. Decorators who work out of their homes can usually give your cake more time and personalized attention if your birthday child's heart is set on having a particular type of decorated cake. The price may be less expensive than a bakery, and the cake will probably taste better, too.

❑ Hiring a professional clown or magician may be out of your price range, but do you know an aspiring entertainer who would provide the entertainment at a reasonable price? Another entertainment idea is to ask a friend with a special talent such as a potter or gourmet cook to do demonstrations or lead the kids in fun learning activities.

❑ When funds are low, use bartering to get what you need for the party. Work with other parents to swap skills and services you can provide such as babysitting, housecleaning, or housesitting for services they can provide for your party such as cake decorating, entertainment, use of their pool, etc.

❑ Look for free or low-cost activities that could serve as the theme and entertainment for the party. Does your city have a children's museum? Coordinate your child's party to take advantage of any special museum programs. Is a local church hosting a free puppet show? Take the group to see it and then go to a local park for a picnic lunch and birthday cake afterward.

❑ While we're on the topic of saving on birthday parties, don't forget that your children will probably be invited to many parties throughout the year. Maintaining a stockpile of gifts you've found on sale is a great way to save money on presents for these parties. See pages 10-12 of Chapter One: *Meaningful Gift Giving* for more information on starting your own gift shelf.

Avoiding Birthday Party Letdown

Before we end this discussion of children's birthday parties, let's address the issue of dealing with a history of birthday extravagance. What should you do if your children are accustomed to elaborate birthday parties but you want to simplify? This scenario is similar to the one we discussed in Chapter Three: *Saint Valentine's Day Simplified*. However, this situation is a bit more challenging because children may have a harder time understanding why you want to scale back.

Communication is key as you work to make changes in the way you celebrate. Talk with your child about his perception of a great party. What does he feel is essential in making the birthday memorable? As you identify what is most important to your child, look for low-cost alternatives to achieve the same results. If having a character theme party is crucial, compromise by limiting the rest of the party to cake and ice cream and activities that are free. If a skating party is what he really wants, agree to have a party at the roller rink but limit the guest list to only a few close friends.

> Creating an inexpensive party that wows your child just as much as an elaborate one may require an all-out creative effort on your part.

Another thing to keep in mind is that you may need to scale back in phases rather than all at once. Going from lavish to simple in the course of one year may require too much of an adjustment. Take your simplification in phases so your child can ease into the idea that simpler celebrations can be just as fun. First try scaling back the expense of one aspect of the party such as the guest list. Next year tackle the simplification of activities and party food.

Realize, too, that creating an inexpensive party that wows your child just as much as an elaborate one may require an all-out creative effort on your part. Concentrate on economical ideas that make a big splash. This is where the input of other parents is helpful. Ask what worked well for them in birthday bashes they have hosted on a conservative budget.

One last suggestion is to make your older child feel special by giving her a great deal of control over the planning process. Set a budget for the party and offer suggestions, but let her make the decisions on how the money is spent. The added benefit of this approach is that the child receives a valuable lesson on budgeting in the process. Even if less is spent on the party than in years past, your young person will probably enjoy it more because she had the privilege and responsibility of choosing exactly how to spend it.

Alternative Ideas for Celebrating Anniversaries

This chapter is dedicated to birthday and anniversary celebrations, but so far, not much has been said about anniversaries. Not that anniversaries are any less worthy of celebration, but birthdays naturally receive more fanfare and hoopla. After all, everyone has a birthday but not everyone has an anniversary. Typically, parents put a great deal of time and energy into throwing birthday bashes for their children while letting their own wedding anniversaries slip by quietly and uneventfully.

With the exception of milestone anniversaries (e.g., 25th, 50th, 75th), wedding anniversaries are usually celebrated privately by just the husband and wife. Many times these celebrations consist of going out for a nice dinner or enjoying a short getaway. However, the cost of such an excursion can be prohibitive for couples on a budget. Below you will find some cost-efficient ideas for commemorating your wedding date in a way that is meaningful to you.

❑ Plant a tree together as a symbol of your growing marriage. Take pictures of yourselves beside the tree on each subsequent anniversary. As the tree grows bigger and stronger, it will serve as a visual reminder that your relationship is also changing and growing each year.

❑ Take a walk down memory lane by revisiting the church where your wedding was held, the reception hall, or the place you celebrated your honeymoon. Spend time reciting your original vows or write some new ones for the anniversary occasion.

❑ Plan a romantic evening for your spouse during which you recreate a portion of your honeymoon experience. Decorate the house to make it look like the place where you spent your honeymoon. Serve foods you ate during your trip. Display pictures from your honeymoon or wear a piece of clothing or jewelry you wore. For fun, create a honeymoon trivia game to test your spouse's memory of those first precious days of marriage.

❑ Celebrate your anniversary by doing whatever you did on your first date. Go to a movie, grab a burger from the burger joint, go roller skating—whatever you did on your first official date. Throughout the evening, talk about details each of you remembers from that date.

❑ Rather than going to a restaurant for dinner together, why not enjoy a picnic meal? Keep it cheap by packing your own picnic basket, or splurge a little by buying precooked foods from a deli. Take along a big blanket and a box of old photos to look through while you savor your meal.

❑ If you'd like to celebrate with a short trip but think you can't afford it, inquire at a nearby state park about renting a cabin for a few days. Not only are the rates usually very reasonable, but you can also save money by taking along your own food and enjoying all the free things the park has to offer for entertainment.

❑ If going out for a romantic dinner is out of the question because you can't afford the meal and a babysitter, try having your candlelit dinner at home. Set up a card table and chairs in your bedroom or some other part of the house you don't usually use for eating. Use your best china, flatware and tablecloth. Keep the meal simple or cook up an exotic new recipe for the occasion. Put the kids to bed early, light the candles and enjoy a quiet meal without any distractions from your little ones.

❏ Another twist on the idea above is to enjoy an early morning breakfast on your own patio or deck. Watch the sunrise while you sip flavored coffee and nibble on your favorite breakfast foods. This is good for couples who are early birds. If you worry about the kids waking while you're out on the deck, hook up a baby monitor so you can hear them if they need you.

❏ Instead of dining out for a full meal, treat yourselves to an anniversary dessert. Have a picnic or eat a light meal at home beforehand, and then go to an establishment known for its decadent dessert selection. Share one large dessert or order two different selections for you both to sample.

If you need help planning a milestone anniversary celebration, reread Chapter Six: *Simplifying the Wedding Celebration* for helpful hints. Many of the ideas for saving money on weddings and receptions would work equally well in planning a 25th, 50th or 75th anniversary celebration. For help in planning a more casual anniversary party, read back over the list of birthday party ideas to stimulate your creativity. There is no particular protocol for bringing people together to celebrate a couple's anniversary. Many of those fun birthday ideas would work well if done with an anniversary twist.

Birthday and Anniversary Gift Ideas

Birthday and anniversary gifts come in every size, shape and personality, just like the people who celebrate birthdays and anniversaries. Some gifts are useful, while others are fanciful. Some gifts are intended to be fun while others are given with practicality in mind.

Throughout this book, you will find a plethora of gift ideas. The beauty of most of these ideas is their versatility. Certainly most low-cost Christmas gift ideas are appropriate for birthdays, too. Mother's and Father's Day gift ideas would also work for anniversaries. For your convenience, I have included a master list of over 100 gift ideas culled from the other chapters plus a few new ones to help you select meaningful gifts for all the anniversaries and birthdays you encounter throughout the year. Remember that although there is a special section just for children, many of the other ideas can be adapted if the birthday boy or girl is under the age of 18.

~ *Master List of Gift Ideas* ~

Homemade Gifts

❑ Make a scrapbook of the history of your relationship with the birthday person or of the anniversary couple's relationship together. Fill it with pictures, mementos and memories from the past.

❑ Give the birthday person handmade bath products. Check the library or Internet to find recipes for homemade bath oils, bath salts, bubble bath and soaps.

❑ Using your computer, create a Certificate of Appreciation to honor the recipient for the important role he plays in your life.

❑ Put your artistic abilities to work and create a piece of art—a song, painting, sketch or poem—in honor of the recipient's special day.

❑ Create a webpage devoted to the honoree. Include family photos and descriptions of the person's unique qualities and accomplishments. Once you've uploaded the site, include the website address in a card telling the recipient to surf to that site for a surprise.

❑ Using a desktop publishing program, type up the recipient's favorite poem and add graphics. Put it in an attractive frame.

❑ Is there some old comedian or sitcom that always makes the honoree chuckle? Use your VCR to make a tape of as many episodes as you can record.

❑ Use your computer to make a family cookbook with recipes contributed by different family members. Or make a cookbook of all of your own special recipes to share with the celebrant.

❑ Try your hand at making homemade potpourri or scented candles. Check out a book from the library on this topic or search the Internet for instructions.

❑ If you have artistic flair, purchase blank note cards with envelopes. Decorate the cards with your own drawings to make personalized note cards for the recipient.

❑ If you can knit or crochet, make the honoree a new scarf, hat, afghan or pair of mittens. If you sew, create a new apron, fleece throw or keepsake pillow.

❑ Make an "I Love You because..." or "You're Special because..." jar. On individual slips of paper, write something you love and appreciate about the honoree. Place the slips of paper in a decorative jar. You can also make an "I Love You" book by writing each thought on a different page of a blank journal.

❑ If you are handy with a needle and embroidery floss, create a cross-stitch sampler featuring a quote or Bible verse that is particularly meaningful. Or use your calligraphy skills and put the finished product in an attractive frame.

❑ Make a family calendar that includes family birthdays, anniversaries, holidays and other special occasions. Decorate it with family photos or children's artwork.

❑ Use fabric paint or iron-on transfers for your inkjet printer to create a personalized apron or tote bag. Embellish it with transfers of family photos, or paint on stenciled decorations.

❑ Children's handprints or footprints make a memorable gift for a parent or grandparent. Make an impression of the child's hand in modeling clay to make a wall hanging or quick drying cement to make a garden stepping stone. You can also use washable ink or paint to stamp the child's handprint or footprint onto cardstock.

Homemade Food Gifts

❑ Make 2 batches of the recipient's favorite cookies: one batch to enjoy now, one batch wrapped tightly in freezer bags to be frozen for later.

❑ Make a basket containing a variety of homemade jams, jellies, relishes or pickles. Give several of these as your gift or give just one along with a loaf of homemade bread.

❑ Give homemade bread or muffins in a decorative gift tin or a basket with a bow. If you like, include the recipe so if the recipient enjoys your gift, she can make more later.

❑ Give a gift basket of homemade flavored coffees, creamers and hot cocoa. If this gift is for an anniversary, include a set of matching mugs for the husband and wife to use as they enjoy the gift together.

❑ If the honoree has an obsession with chocolate, fill a gift basket with several varieties of homemade chocolate cookies, candy, and brownies. If the recipient loves sweets but is concerned about weight gain, use recipes for goodies that are low in fat and calories.

❑ Search the Internet for recipes for cookie, muffin and pancake mixes that you can give in decorative jars for the honoree to make and enjoy later.

❑ Make an ordinary food extraordinary. Whip up a heart-shaped homemade pizza, a giant-sized cookie, or a specially decorated cake in an interesting shape.

Embellished Store-Bought Gifts

❑ Have an enlargement made of a special family photo. Put it in an inexpensive frame and present it with a note about a special memory you have from the day the photo was taken.

❑ Make a keepsake video containing something that would be special to the recipient: his children singing songs, friends telling why they love him, or you reminiscing times you've shared together.

❑ Make a gift basket or bag filled with samples and other inexpensive items from dollar stores. Go with a particular theme or include a collection of miscellaneous useful items. For gift basket theme ideas, see pages 14-15.

- ❑ Make a personalized comic book. Fill an inexpensive photo album with pictures of family and friends. Write funny captions to go with each picture.
- ❑ Give the recipient the gift of curling up with a good book. Purchase some reading material you know he'll enjoy; include a mug and some herbal tea or flavored coffee.
- ❑ Embellish an ordinary picture frame with paint, sequins, or other decorations. Fill the frame with artwork done by the recipient's children or grandchildren.

Gifts of Your Time

- ❑ Write an IOU for something the recipient usually pays to have done such as yard work, babysitting, or basic car maintenance.
- ❑ Make a book of coupons for free massages, evenings of undivided attention, or nights off from cooking, etc. These ideas work well if the recipient is your spouse. If not, give coupons for cutting grass, weeding flowerbeds, or washing the car.
- ❑ Give the recipient the gift of time off from normal household duties. Write a promissory note stating that for the next week or month you promise to take care of a certain household chore for which the recipient is usually responsible.
- ❑ Arrange for the honoree to experience a relaxing overnight getaway to see friends or relatives. If the honoree is your spouse, take the kids to Grandma's for the weekend so your loved one can enjoy a few days of quiet rest and relaxation alone at home.
- ❑ Offer to help out with a task that needs more than one person to complete: painting, cleaning out the attic or landscaping.
- ❑ Create a romantic meal in the anniversary couple's own home. Cook up a special meal and bring it over. Set the table and put the food out so they can serve themselves. Light the candles and then vamoose so they can enjoy a candlelit dinner for two.

❑ Give the person a day of fun. Go window shopping, hit some yard sales or visit antique stores—whatever the honoree would enjoy. While you're out, pick up an inexpensive lunch or pack a picnic to share in the park.

❑ If the birthday person is your spouse, help her pamper herself with a long, luxurious bath. Run the water for her and set out the best towels. Light candles, dim the lights and make a cup of her favorite warm beverage. Be available in case she needs anything.

❑ Devote a few days of your time to spring cleaning for the honoree. Do all those time-consuming cleaning tasks that usually get done only once a year.

❑ Volunteer a day or several days of your time to complete those tasks the recipient cannot do or cannot afford to pay someone else to do such as pruning trees or cleaning out the gutters.

❑ Do a week or month's worth of cooking for the recipients. Fill their freezer with homemade meals that they can easily heat and serve rather than have to cook.

Inexpensive Store-Bought Gifts

❑ Check out the clearance table or bargain bookrack at your local bookstore. Find a book on a topic of interest to the recipient.

❑ Check the video rental shop for sales on pre-owned copies of movies the birthday person or anniversary couple would enjoy.

❑ Shop at used bookstores, thrift shops or garage sales for gently used items that would make great gifts: a book by a favorite author, back issues of a favorite magazine, a vintage hat or purse.

❑ Give the celebrant a rose bush to plant in her flowerbed so she can enjoy fresh flowers for years to come.

❑ Does the recipient collect something as a hobby? Purchase an item to add to the collection. Or if purchasing a collectible is too expensive, give the honoree something that relates to the hobby, such as a book on the topic.

Practical, Non-Cluttering Gifts

Personal Care Products
- ❑ Perfume
- ❑ Hand and body lotions
- ❑ Makeup
- ❑ Bath products (soaps, bath oils, shower gel, bubble bath)
- ❑ Nail care items (nail polish, cuticle cream, etc.)

Store-Bought Food Gifts
- ❑ Fruit and nuts
- ❑ Flavored breads or bread mixes
- ❑ Wine, champagne, liqueur
- ❑ Flavored oils and vinegar
- ❑ Gourmet coffees and teas
- ❑ Gourmet sauces and flavorings
- ❑ Flavored coffees and creamers
- ❑ Hot cocoa mixes
- ❑ Unusual varieties of pasta
- ❑ Gourmet spices
- ❑ Ice cream toppings
- ❑ Chocolate

Household Items
- ❑ Stationery and stamps
- ❑ Candles
- ❑ Long distance phone cards
- ❑ Film or disposable cameras
- ❑ Recipe cards
- ❑ A computer program the recipient would use
- ❑ Dishcloths, bath towels, sheets and pillowcases

Miscellaneous Consumable Gifts
- ❑ Flowers
- ❑ Plants or flower bulbs
- ❑ Birdseed
- ❑ Magazine or newspaper subscriptions
- ❑ Calendars

Gifts of Experience
Gift Certificates
- ☐ Restaurant
- ☐ Grocery store
- ☐ Department or clothing store
- ☐ Specialty store
- ☐ Hardware store or home improvement center
- ☐ Movie theater or video rental
- ☐ Yogurt or ice cream shop
- ☐ Entertainment coupon books
- ☐ Manicure, pedicure, facial or massage
- ☐ Classes offered on topics related to his/her interests or hobbies

Memberships and Season Passes
- ☐ Zoo or aquarium
- ☐ Opera, symphony or community theater
- ☐ YMCA or health club
- ☐ Amusement park
- ☐ Art museum
- ☐ Botanical gardens

Tickets
- ☐ Sporting events
- ☐ Concerts
- ☐ Exhibitions
- ☐ Theater productions
- ☐ Festivals
- ☐ Seminars
- ☐ Hot air balloon or helicopter rides

Inexpensive Store-Bought Gifts for Young People
- ☐ Encourage creativity by giving new crayons, markers, an art pad, sidewalk chalk, construction paper, stickers, glitter, etc.
- ☐ Give the child a disposable camera along with a promise to pay for film developing after all the pictures are taken.

❑ Girls of all ages like to pamper and beautify themselves. Give a gift basket containing body spray, lip gloss, nail polish and shower gel.

❑ Introduce the birthday child to the joys of stamp collecting. The US Postal Service sells stamp collecting kits, or you can purchase them from hobby stores.

❑ Enlarge a treasured photo of the teen hanging out with best friends or doing something memorable like making the winning score. Put the photograph in an attractive frame to be displayed in the honoree's room.

❑ Children love bubbles. Give the birthday child a large bottle of bubble solution and a selection of bubble wands.

❑ Is there a particular craft or hobby the young person enjoys or would enjoy if she learned how to do it? Fill a box with a variety of supplies needed to do that craft.

Homemade Gifts for Young People

❑ Fill a large basket with the young person's favorite homemade cookies or candy. Include a note stating that the container may be returned for refills throughout the year.

❑ Give the child several different colors of homemade Play-Doh®. Include a set of inexpensive cookie cutters to use with it. Search the Internet or check out craft books from the library for recipes.

❑ Put together a dress-up box containing a collection of adult party clothes, hats, costume jewelry, scarves and purses.

❑ Create a "Book about Me" by decorating an inexpensive journal. Write a variety of statements on the blank pages such as, "When I grow up, I want to be..." or "What I like best about myself is..." Include a new pen or mechanical pencil for the recipient to use when completing the questions.

❑ Give a homemade gift certificate for a free trip to the ice cream shop or the child's favorite video arcade. You foot the bill and provide transportation.

❑ Use your computer to make a beginner's cookbook filled with recipes for all the teen's favorite dishes plus a few new ones. When the honoree moves away from home, he can take it with him to help recreate the tastes of home.

❑ Make the birthday child a personalized brag book. Fill a mini-photo album with photos of friends, family, pets and accomplishments she has achieved.

❑ Start a tradition of giving the birthday child a Christmas ornament each year. When she moves away from home someday, she will have her own collection of special ornaments to take with her.

❑ Make a tape recording of yourself reading stories, singing songs, or reciting nursery rhymes that you know the child would enjoy.

❑ Put your creative writing and artistic skills to work to create a personalized book of a fun make-believe story starring the birthday child. Add a tape recording of the story if the child is not yet able to read.

❑ Give homemade coupons redeemable for things your young person would enjoy such as getting to stay up past their regular bedtime or an afternoon of window shopping at the mall.

Chapter Ten:
Conclusion

*W*hat if you need help with a holiday such as Independence Day or a special occasion like a housewarming party that we haven't discussed? Throughout these chapters, I addressed only major holidays and life events. Without a doubt, any special occasion—whether mentioned in this book or not—has the potential of getting out of hand and losing its significance if not celebrated simply and in a manner that is meaningful to you.

If you find yourself in this predicament, my advice is to identify exactly what it is about the particular event that causes you stress and then reread the sections of *Celebrate Simply* that deal with those issues. For your convenience, I have listed the major categories of holiday anxiety below. Under each general category, you will find related topics with corresponding page numbers where you can find pertinent information for dealing with that type of stress.

~ *Index of Holiday Stress Factors* ~

Chapter Eleven:
Resources

Gift Giving Resources
Related Books
- ❑ *Handmade Gifts Under $10* by Anne Van Wagner Childs, Editor (Leisure Arts 1998).
- ❑ *The Complete Guide to Creative Gift Giving* by Cynthia G. Yates (Servant Publications 1997).
- ❑ *Gifts of Good Taste: Yummy Recipes and Creative Crafts* by Anne Van Wagner Childs, Editor (Leisure Arts 1999).
- ❑ *Gifts from the Kitchen: Recipes and Ideas for Take-Along Gifts* by Wilton Enterprises (Wilton 1995).

Related Websites
- ❑ *RichGiving.com: Giving Meaningful Gifts* - This site emphasizes "ways to give of yourself, give for the soul and give for the future." http://www.richgiving.com
- ❑ *The Center for a New American Dream* - "Helping Americans consume responsibly to protect the environment, enhance quality of life and promote social justice." Check out the page dedicated to simplifying holidays and gift giving. http://www.newdream.org
- ❑ *ShopConsciously* - "Toward a Peaceful and Prosperous Planet." The goal of this site is to promote the belief that environmental responsibility is smart business. ShopConsciously brings together shoppers who care with artists, artisans and business people who care. Shop this site for gifts and products that are people friendly, earth friendly, beautiful and socially kind. http://www.shopconsciously.com

Christmas Resources
Related Books

❑ *Unplug The Christmas Machine: A Complete Guide to Putting Love and Joy Back into the Season* by Jo Robinson and Jean Coppock Staeheli (Quill 1991).

❑ *Hundred Dollar Holiday: The Case for a Joyful Christmas* by Bill McKibben (Simon & Schuster 1998).

❑ *Debt Proof Your Holidays* by Mary Hunt (St. Martin's Press 1997).

❑ *Christmas Gifts under $10* by Anne Van Wagner Childs, Editor (Leisure Arts 1997).

❑ *Christmas Gifts of Good Taste* by Anne Van Wagner Childs, Editor (Leisure Arts 1991). [Note: Leisure Arts now has a series of *Christmas Gifts of Good Taste* books. Any one of these annual editions is sure to be a winner.]

❑ *Christ in Christmas: A Family Advent Celebration* by Dr. James Dobson, et al. (Navpress 1989).

❑ *Advent: Worship and Activities for Families* by Margaret Anne Huffman (Abingdon Press 1998).

❑ *Simplify and Celebrate: Embracing the Soul of Christmas Alternatives* by Alternatives for Simple Living (Northstone 1997).

❑ *Treasury of Celebrations* by Alternatives for Simple Living (Northstone 1997).

❑ *Whose Birthday Is It Anyway? Ideas for a Christ-Centered Holiday* (Alternatives for Simple Living). This annual guide comes in various denominational versions. A promotion kit is also available to help raise interest and awareness in your church or parish. Note that it can only be purchased through Alternatives for Simple Living. (Call 1-800-821-6153 or order online at: http://www.simpleliving.org/)

❑ *Frozen Assets: How to Cook for a Day and Eat for a Month* by Deborah Taylor-Hough (Champion Press 1998). This book will help you simplify the Christmas season by teaching you how to cook and freeze meals beforehand for use during the busy holiday season.

❑ *Frozen Assets Lite and Easy: How to Cook for a Day and Eat for a Month* by Deborah Taylor-Hough (Champion Press 2002). This book is the low-calorie version of the book listed above.

Related Websites
❑ *The Center for a New American Dream* - "Helping Americans consume responsibly to protect the environment, enhance quality of life and promote social justice." Check out the page dedicated to simplifying holidays. http://www.newdream.org

❑ *Alternatives for Simple Living* - "Equipping people of faith to challenge consumerism, live justly and celebrate responsibly." This site has a vast library of articles as well as many quality publications available for purchase. http://www.simpleliving.org/

❑ *Emanuel Lutheran Church Chrismon Project* (Santa Barbara, CA) - This church has an absolutely beautiful collection of Chrismons that they share in pictures on their website. These Chrismons may be more intricate than you want to attempt, but will definitely provide you with ideas for making your own. http://emanuel.netministries.org/chrismon.html

❑ *Aldersgate United Methodist Church Chrismon page* (Durham, NC) - Another church website that contains pictures of their own Chrismon tree as well as links to lists of common Chrismon symbols and their meanings. http://www.aldersgate.org/chrismons.htm

❑ *ChristianCrafters.com* - This site contains information about making Chrismons and ornaments for a Jesse tree, as well as many other crafts with a Christian theme. http://www.christiancrafters.com/

Valentine's Day Resources
Related Books
❑ *The RoMANtic's Guide: Hundred's of Tips for a Lifetime of Love* by Michael Webb (Hyperion 2000).

❑ *Dating Your Mate* by Rick Bundschuh and Dave Gilbert (Harvest House 1987).

❑ *Creative Dating* by Doug Fields and Todd Temple (Oliver Nelson 1986).

Related Websites

❑ *The RoMANtic* - This site is maintained by Michael Webb, the man who has been dubbed as the world's most romantic husband. Here you will find "thousands of creative ideas and expert advice on love, dating and romance." http://www.theromantic.com

❑ *LovingYou.com's Romantic Ideas* - "Love, Life and Romance." This section of the LovingYou.com site claims to have over 1,200 romantic ideas submitted by website visitors. http://romance.lovingyou.com/ideas/

❑ *Romantic-Tips.com* - "Romantic Tips and Ideas for Romance". This site also contains a large collection of ideas for romantic inspiration. http://www.romantic-tips.com/

Easter Resources
Related Books

❑ *A Christ-Centered Easter: Day-By-Day Activities to Celebrate Easter Week* by Janet Hales and Joe Hales (Eagle Gate 2002).

❑ *Celebrate Jesus at Easter: Family Devotions for Ash Wednesday Through Easter* by Kimberly Ingalls Reese (Concordia Publishing House 2002).

❑ *Before and After Easter: Activities and Ideas for Lent to Pentecost* by Debbie Trafton O'Neal (Augsburg Fortress Publishers 2001).

❑ *Treasury of Celebrations* by Alternatives for Simple Living (Northstone 1997).

❑ *Treasury of Easter Celebrations* by Julie K. Hogan (Ideals Publications 2002).

❑ *Why Celebrate Easter?* by Steve Russo (Broadman and Holman 2001).

Related Websites

❑ *Alternatives for Simple Living* - "Equipping people of faith to challenge consumerism, live justly and celebrate responsibly." Check out the information about Easter celebrations. http://www.simpleliving.org/

❑ *Christian Seder: Passover Dinner for Christian Congregations* - This site contains information and links to help you plan a Christian seder as part of your Easter celebration. http://www.christianseder.com/

Mother's Day and Father's Day Resources
Related Websites

❑ *Holidays on the Net* - "Your Source for Holiday Celebrations on the World Wide Web." Check out the "Mother's Day on the Net" and "Father's Day on the Net" pages for craft and celebration ideas. http://www.holidays.net/mother/ and http://www.holidays.net/father/

❑ *Everything Mother's Day* - Maintained by its parent site, EverythingHolidays.com, this site has a nice collection of information and links related to Mother's Day. [By the way, the EverythingHolidays.com is a good source for information on other major holidays, but ironically, they didn't have an "Everything Father's Day" page at the time of this writing!] http://www.everythingmothersday.com/

Wedding Resources
Related Books

❑ *Bridal Bargains: Secrets to Throwing a Fantastic Wedding on a Realistic Budget* by Denise and Alan Fields (Windsor Peak Press 2000).

❑ *The Budget Wedding Sourcebook* by Madeline Barillo (McGraw-Hill/Contemporary Books 2000).

- ❏ *How to Have a Big Wedding on a Small Budget: Cut Your Wedding Costs by Half or More* by Diane Warner (Betterway Publications 1997).
- ❏ *The Alternative Wedding Book* by Alternatives for Simple Living (Northstone 1997).

Related Websites

- ❏ *WedFrugal.com* - "The Frugal Wedding Site: Helping You Save Money on the Costs of Your Wedding." Maintained by Rachel Sanfordlyn Shreckengast, this site has a wealth of good information on cutting wedding costs. http://wedfrugal.com/
- ❏ *FrugalBride.com* - "Canada's First Frugal Bride Website." If you live in Canada, you can search for vendors in your area. The rest of us can look for wedding tips and craft ideas, use the site's planning tools, or chat with other "babbling brides" on the Babbling Brides Bulletin Boards. http://www.frugalbride.com/
- ❏ *ShoestringWeddings.com* - This site caters to couples with "big dreams, small budgets." Here you'll find ideas and a nice collection of wedding craft instructions. http://www.shoestringweddings.com/

Halloween Resources
Related Books
- ❏ *Family Celebrations at Thanksgiving: And Alternatives to Halloween* by Ann Hibbard (Baker Book House 1995).
- ❏ *Halloween: What's a Christian to Do?* by Steve Russo (Harvest House 1998).

Related Websites
- ❏ *Halloween Outreach* - This ministry of Joshua Outreach Group is dedicated to "exposing darkness by sharing the light." The website contains information and materials for purchase to help you share your faith during Halloween. http://www.halloweenoutreach.com

❑ *United States Fund of UNICEF* - Here you can find more information on the *Trick-or-Treat for UNICEF* project. http://www.unicefusa.org/trickortreat/index.html

❑ *FamilyCorner.com* - "Giving 'Time-out' a New Meaning." This site has all kinds of helpful family information with a particularly rich collection of costume ideas. http://www.thefamilycorner.com/

Thanksgiving Resources
Related Books

❑ *Celebrations of a Nation: Early American Holidays* by Lucille Johnston (Candel Publishing 2001).

❑ *Family Celebrations at Thanksgiving: And Alternatives to Halloween* by Ann Hibbard (Baker Book House 1995).

Related Websites

❑ *Plimoth-on-Web* - Presented by Plimoth Plantation, "The Living History Museum of 17th Century Plymouth." Here you'll find an enormous amount of historical data on America's earliest settlers. http://www.plimoth.org/

Birthday and Anniversary Resources
Related Books

❑ *Birthday Parties: Best Party Tips and Ideas* by Vicki Lansky (Book Peddlers 1995).

❑ *Clever Party Planning: Party Planning Ideas and Themes for Kids, Teens, and Adults* by Suzanne Singleton (Twenty Nine Angels Publishing 1999).

❑ *Wedding Anniversary Idea Book* by Rayburn Ray and Rose Ray (JM Productions 1995).

Related Websites

❑ *BirthdayPartyIdeas.com* - This website claims to have the "world's largest collection of party ideas" (over 3,200 of them). If your party-planning creativity needs a little boost, check out this expansive list of ideas submitted by visitors. http://www.birthdaypartyideas.com/

❑ *The Dollar Stretcher* - "Living Better for Less." This site has a topical index that you can search for articles and ideas on a huge variety of topics, including saving on birthday and anniversary celebrations. http://www.stretcher.com/

Resources on Miscellaneous Topics
Holiday Activities for the Whole Family
❑ *Let's Make a Memory* by Gloria Gaither and Shirley Dobson (Word Publishing 1994).

❑ *Kids' Holiday Fun: Great Family Activities Every Month of the Year* by Penny Warner (Meadowbrook Press 1997).

Stimulating Your Creativity
❑ *A Whack on the Side of the Head: How You Can Be More Creative* by Roger Von Oech (Warner Books 1998).

❑ *A Kick in the Seat of the Pants: Using Your Explorer, Artist, Judge and Warrior to Be More Creative* by Roger Von Oech (HarperCollins 1986).

❑ *Jump Start Your Brain* by Doug Hall and David Wecker (Warner Books 1996).

Simple, Frugal, Debt-Free Living
❑ *The Complete Tightwad Gazette: Promoting Thrift as a Viable Alternative Lifestyle* by Amy Dacyczyn (Random House 1999).

❑ *Financial Peace: Restoring Financial Hope to You and Your Family* by Dave Ramsey and Sharon Ramsey (Viking 1997).

❑ *Your Money or Your Life: Transforming Your Relationship with Money and Achieving Financial Independence* by Joe Dominguez and Vicki Robin (Penguin 1999).

Resources

- *The Richest Man in Babylon* by George S. Clason (Reissue edition: Signet 2002).
- *Miserly Moms: Living on One Income in a Two-Income Economy* by Jonni McCoy (Bethany House 2001).
- *Frugal Families: Making the Most of Your Hard-Earned Money* by Jonni McCoy (Bethany House 2003).
- *Debt-Proof Living* by Mary Hunt (Broadman & Holman 1998).
- *Cheap Talk with the Frugal Friends: Over 600 Tips, Tricks, and Creative Ideas for Saving Money* by Angie Zalewski and Deana Ricks (Starburst 2001).
- *A Simple Choice: A Practical Guide to Saving Your Time, Money and Sanity* by Deborah Taylor-Hough (Champion Press 2000).
- *Shop, Save and Share* by Ellie Kaye (Bethany House 1998).

Index

Index

H

I

Index

Give the Gift of Simpler, More Meaningful Celebrations to Your Loved Ones

PURCHASE ADDITIONAL COPIES OF THIS BOOK FROM LEADING BOOKSTORES OR ORDER HERE

❑ YES! I want _____ copies of *Celebrate Simply: Your Guide to Simpler, More Meaningful Holidays and Special Occasions.* I have enclosed **$12.95 plus $3.50 shipping and handling** for each copy ordered and shipped within the US.

I have enclosed a check or money order for $ _____.

Name _____

Address _____

City/State/Zip _____

Phone _____ E-mail address _____

Please make your check or money order payable to *"Celebrate Simply"* and return it with a copy of this form to:

Celebrate Simply
8715 Brucewood Lane
Knoxville, TN 37923-6035

FOR INTERNATIONAL ORDERS OR TO PAY USING YOUR CREDIT CARD, ORDER ONLINE AT:
http://www.celebratesimply.com
or call **1-800-318-5725**

Feedback, Please!

Did this book help you on your journey to simpler celebrations? Do you have simplification ideas of your own that you'd like to share? We'd love to hear your story.

Send your letters to:
Celebrate Simply
Attn: Nancy Twigg
8715 Brucewood Lane
Knoxville, TN 37923-6035

Send e-mail correspondence to:
nancy@celebratesimply.com

Please submit errors and corrections to:
editor@celebratesimply.com

Submissions cannot be returned and become property of *Celebrate Simply*. Please include your name, address and e-mail address with your submission so that we may contact you for permission to use your submission in future editions of *Celebrate Simply*.

About the Author

When Nancy and Michael Twigg both left comfortable jobs to test the murky waters of self-employment in 1997, simple living became a must. Soon after this major life change, Nancy began publishing her *Counting the Cost* newsletter to share and exchange ideas with other frugal families. For the first few years of publication, *Counting the Cost* was a printed newsletter; later it became the free e-mail newsletter it is today.

In addition to writing and editing *Counting the Cost*, Nancy's work has been published in several national Christian magazines and newsletters, and she has been featured in numerous radio and television interviews. She currently appears in the weekly "Simple Saver" segment on WBIR-TV's *Style: A Show for You* (Knoxville, Tennessee).

To learn more about simple and frugal living or to subscribe to *Counting the Cost* newsletter, visit Nancy online at www.countingthecost.com. Nancy is also available to speak to groups of all sizes on topics related to simple and frugal Christian living and celebrating. To schedule a seminar for your church, homeschool or women's group, contact Nancy via email at nancy@countingthecost.com or by mail at Counting the Cost Publications, 8715 Brucewood Lane, Knoxville TN 37923.